About the Author

Maxine is a mother and grandmother who has had thirty odd years working with spirit. She is a spiritual teacher, healer, and psychic medium. Working alongside her guide, Running Bear, they have devised this book together, sharing their special moments of magic to help heal others. She shares her vulnerable moments and how spirit helped her in time of need. This book will help you to look for the magic that will help you on your self-love journey.

The Spiritual Guide How to:
I Love Me

WITH Love

M.K. Booker

M. K. Booker

The Spiritual Guide How To: I Love Me

Olympia Publishers
London

www.olympiapublishers.com
OLYMPIA PAPERBACK EDITION

A CIP catalogue record for this title is
available from the British Library.

ISBN: 978-1-80074-622-0

First Published in 2023

Olympia Publishers
Tallis House
2 Tallis Street
London
EC4Y 0AB

Printed in Great Britain

Dedication

I dedicate this book to my loving Nanny Vi and my father, Keith, who have both encouraged me to write this book.

Loving yourself is not a selfish act, it is the most important relationship you will ever have.

The way you feel about yourself will impact every aspect of your life, including relationships and health. Loving yourself is the key to finding your happiness.

Throughout my life, the painful moments, no matter how dark they were, I see them as a valuable lesson that has helped me grow into the kind, caring person I am today.

I have written this book to share the lesson I have learned, which will provide you with some guidance and inspiration.

If you focus on the HURT, you will continue to suffer.
If you focus on the LESSON, you will continue to grow.
Shahida Majeed

Introduction

Many of you have heard the phrase, "No one is ever going to love you until you love yourself." In other words, until you start to love yourself unconditionally, no one else will. Love thrives when we give it to other people, too many can provide it but find it challenging to love yourselves.

Countless of you find you are the hardest person to love. We all know what mistakes we have made, so it makes sense that we criticise ourselves more harshly than anyone else. Many of us have unknowingly started forming a dependency and seeking approval from unhealthy situations that lead to a downward spiral to sadness and pain.

You may be asking what qualifies me to write this book, the only qualifications I hold are a BSc Hons in Psychology and another in Business and IT. Neither of these courses taught me how to love myself, it was only through my life lessons and spirit that I realised that I needed to open my heart to myself.

I class myself as a mature lady who has been fortunate enough to be blessed with a beautiful gift. I have always been able to sense, feel, and see spirit since I was a small child.

For the first forty years of my life, I had experienced all kinds of abuse from men, women, friends, and family. I thought people being cruel to me was my norm. As a small child, both parents neglected me, and my peers bullied me at school. At the age of six, I was told by a nasty man who liked to inflict sexual and physical pain on me that I deserved horrible things to happen to me as I was so "ugly." The pain and these cruel words haunted me throughout the first part of my life. Consequently, having an abusive childhood, I ended up in abusive relationships. I went from relationship to relationship seeking someone to love me, as I hated myself.

Experiencing trauma after trauma, losing my father and my baby at the age of twenty-one, then only to be beaten so violently I was left for dead. I naturally lock the pain deep and silently within me, with all the other festering drudge.

But I must admit that there were short periods that glimmered the warmth of the sun that filled my life with laughter, hope, and magic during these darkening times. I had so many beautiful spiritual moments that kept me strong and gave me the willpower to go on.

Turning forty and going through another messy divorce, I could not contain the pain any more.

I had a mental breakdown, for the next several years, I suffered from severe depression. I made various attempts to end my life only to be saved by miracles. In my last effort, the consultant is still puzzled why I am here. He told me whatever God I believed in to thank him as he had performed not only one but two miracles. I should have died, and I should have severe organ failure, but everything was perfect, according to him. At the time, I honestly thought that I could not die. I thought my soul purpose was to endure a torturous life. My mindset told me this was hell, and I deserved every nasty thing that came my way. It was only natural for me to lock myself away from family, friends, and the outside world.

I painted my bedroom black and stayed there for months on end. However, my Angels and loving guide, Running Bear, did not give up on me. Pockets of rainbows started to brighten up my days, which inspired me to begin my spiritual journey. Once I was on this journey, I realised how much hatred I had for people and myself. I was so angry and aggressive. I thought of myself as a massive failure, a rubbish mother to my children, a worthless human being. I had two failed marriages, I thought I was an idiot. Also, my family home was repossessed, which meant there was a high possibility of being homeless.

I became too ill to work; I lost my job.

I was on my own, and there was no one to help me. Unfortunately, the people I had around me loved the fact I had fallen flat onto my face, they revelled in it. Luckily, my beautiful family in spirit helped me find a place to live, but circumstances changed quickly, and again I was faced with being homeless. At this moment, I was terrified. Why is this happening?

I made sure my children had a roof over their heads, but I thought I was generally going to have to sleep on the streets.

I had no friends, no family, and no money. So, I asked my Spiritual Family for help.

You would not believe what happened, next, I was so destitute and afraid that a very unexpected cheque for £1500 landed on my doormat.

It was from the Child Support Agency, backdated maintenance that was owed to me years ago.

With this money, I found a lovely little flat with a nice Landlord. I saw this as a fresh start. I found myself a good job, things looked up until I became seriously ill with only months to live.

Not again, during this time, my employer was not supportive, and they gave me a hard time. Somehow, I know it was spirit, but due to my employer's behaviour, they ended up paying a handsome lump sum of money for me to leave.

As soon as my contract ended, my illness vanished. I heard my inner voice (Spirit) telling me that I only work for them from now on. My beautiful Spiritual Family: Running Bear, my Native American Indian Guide, Angels, other Guides, Spirit Animals, loves ones in spirit, and many more have guided me on my spiritual path.

Everything in my life has changed, I am happy, at peace, respond differently to life challenges with more positivity and a calming reassurance that things will be okay. My family and friends noticeably notice the change in me, I had gone from a ferocious tigress wanting to kill everything in sight to a loving, hippy tree-hugging goddess. How did this incredible transformation happen? I started to love myself, and if I can do it, I know you definitely can.

Even though I have seen and heard spirit from an early age, it was not until I turned forty-seven when I had a huge awakening, experiencing a massive energy shift in my life that made me look within. Running Bear showed me how to start loving myself and told me the importance and how it would impact my life. The very thought of showing myself love was strange and alien to me. This journey that I commenced did not conclude over a day or a week, it took time, and I am still forever learning, but I can honestly say my whole life has changed. I can now see the beauty, the power, and strength not only in me, but also for others that I could not see before, this was a life-changing experience. I have had many harsh lessons throughout my life, experienced all different kinds of abuse, people being nasty and cruel towards me, it seemed endless. But the worst perpetrator of them all was me, I was my own worst enemy.

Does this sound familiar? Are you your own worst enemy? Have you been doing this for years that it has become your norm?

I bet the answer is Yes! Now is the time to break this bad habit and start to allow unconditional love to seep into your heart. Again, if it is possible for me, I know you can start today to transform your life.

Learning how to love yourself is not a selfish act, it is one of the most important lessons you will learn. Some of you may say that you love yourself, but diving deeper within your soul, many of you are hiding and suppressing the ugly within. This book will look at these concepts and provide guidance to help you, most will resonate with you. Go with what is drawing you, let your intuition guide you throughout this book.

A note from your Angel

Open your heart and start your journey now, watch how your world changes around you, inviting love, healthy living, success that all come in a painless, safe, and beautiful way while experiencing happiness, respect, peace, and balance. Start by saying, "I love me."

What Is Unconditional Love?

Unconditional love is the most powerful healing force in the universe, it is known as affection without any limitations or love without conditions. Most parents experience this emotion, loving your children unconditionally, turning it 'on' for yourselves is a different concept. The very first moment you experience unconditional love, you have a transformative moment of feeling acceptance, gratitude, forgiveness, understanding, and respect for who you are.

There are two types of self-love, you have Ego Love, which is narcissism or selfishness, and then there is Unconditionally Love. Ego Love is the ugly side of distorted self-love.

Narcissi's people will only concentrate on themselves, they are consumed with vanity, popularity, power, and success. They take on a persona of a God and tend to look down or criticise others to inflate their Ego. "I love Me" is all about Unconditional Love. Having spoken to many people throughout thirty years of being a Psychic Medium, I have discovered that most people's problems stem from the fact they cannot love themselves. Many of them are in unhappy situations, being abused, controlled, feeling fearful, and petrified of change.

Begin today to transform your life, you deserve to be happy, surrounded by people who love you.

"As I began to love myself, I freed myself of anything that is no good for my health – food, people, things, situations, and

everything that drew me down and away from myself.
At first, I called this attitude a healthy egoism.
Today I know it is 'LOVE OF ONESELF.'
Charlie Chaplin

Why Do We Self-Loath?

There are thousands of reasons we Self-Loath, but the main reason is that we have been conditioned and brainwashed for centuries to hate ourselves.

Having people with low self-esteem, no confidence, etc. is easier for those who want to control and manipulate you.

These people who seek power will bestow their harsh judgment on anyone who does not fit their mould, whether it is down to your skin colour, gender, religion, sexual orientation, size, etc. This has been proven throughout history. For example, countless people were put into slavery due to their skin colour. There has been female mutilation amongst cultures, women not being able to vote, children sweeping chimneys, and the Jews and many others that did not fit Hitler's mould were exterminated.

There is a theory that there is an evil gene, or some people who are not born with a soul, and their sole purpose is to harm others. Hence, we have serial killers, rapists, and other unsavoury characters in this world. Other theorists will argue there is no evil gene, or soulless people, that it is just the way they are treated and down to their environment. Is it genetics, or spiritual? I believe it is a bit of both.

The sad fact some of these people who are cruel to us know no better, as they have come from a brutal and harsh environment. So being abusive to the ones they love is their normal.

For instance, I never met my grandfather on my father's side, all I know is that he was a stringent man, and when my father was a child, if he stepped out of line, his father would give him a serve beating. My father knew no better, he thought this was normal behaviour, and he continued in his father's footsteps, if I were out of line, I too would get a severe beating.

Cruelly treating your loved ones can come from a long linage. However, in this case, it stopped with me as I always vowed to myself when I was young, I would never treat my children the way my parents treated me. So, you can stop this cruel behaviour, this does not have to be your norm.

You can change your behaviour and your action, which we will look at in more detail in the chapter heading "Change Your Reaction."

There are also hereditary factors such as Alcoholism, both men and women abusing the drink only to take it out on those they love.

True Story: Brenda

My mother's friend Brenda was subjected to twenty-five years of domestic violence. Her husband was an alcoholic, and so was his father. He would go to the pub every night, come home, steaming drunk. As soon as he got in, Brenda lay on the floor so he could repeatedly kick her.

At the time, I was a Martial Arts Instructor, and my mother asked me to help her. I asked Brenda why she submissively lay on the floor for him.

She told me that if she refused or put up a fight, it would anger him more, and she would get it worse. I gave Brenda some advice and showed her a couple of easy techniques to use. Literally, two days later, Brenda was around my mother's raging. Her husband had just come home drunk, instead of lying on the floor, she told him NO!

He flared up at her expecting her to be submissive, but no, Brenda turned into a raging wild cat and started to pick things up around her room to throw at him, and what made her even madder was the fact she was only picking up soft items in her rage. Brenda wanted to pick something hard up to hurt him. As for her husband, he was on his knees, cowering and begging her to stop. Brenda stormed out of the house and headed over to my mother to tell her all about it.

After this incident, he no longer raised his hand to her or mistreated her. A few months later, Brenda had the courage, strength, and determination to divorce him.

Most of us have insecurities, with the modern world trying to brainwash us to look and act in specific ways, that we can become prey to those who wish to harm us.

In my early twenties, I was a size ten, slim and beautiful, but when I had two children, my body changed. I was insecure about my weight and how my body looked. My narcissistic husband took advantage of this. I never knew at the time, but I was an attractive young lady who had such a kind soul and fantastic personality that my husband was afraid of someone else coming along to snap me up. Instead of sharing his fear, he made it his mission to make me feel so bad about myself. He literally kept me barefoot and pregnant, trapped and isolated in my own home, and if I did want to venture out, I was too scared. He had convinced me that I was so repulsive throughout the years with his mental abuse, I thought if I went out, people would point and stare at me while making hideous remarks. Maybe some of you can relate to this?

The question was, why do we self-loath? As I have mentioned, there are many reasons, but one of the real reasons is down to the people we had or are still in our lives.

Understanding why they mistreat us gives us some validations and clarification, it is not down to you, your cooking, the way you dress, or how you look.

When they mistreat you, it is not about you, it is about them, their pain, how they are dealing with it, or they are merely just enjoying it.

True Story: Kate

I have a friend called Kate, who had been referred to the acute mental health team and had been sectioned as she tried to kill herself. Kate is a beautiful soul with a heart of gold and would help anyone. All she does is give, give, give.

Unfortunately, her partner is the opposite of her, after giving birth to her second baby, he cheated on Kate.

He told her cruel, horrible things about why he cheated. The sad thing is that she loved him. Tom is her first love, first boyfriend, but throughout their six-year relationship, he played on her insecurities to get what he wanted, and when Tom could not get what he wanted, he went somewhere else. As you can imagine, with this horrible mental abuse, she thinks she is to blame for everything that has gone wrong in her life, her self-esteem, confidence, self-love does not exist. Kate is a stunning woman, and she does not understand why he oppressed her.

From an outside point of view, it is simple; Tom is insecure about his looks and is frightened of losing her to another, so degrading and belittling his beautiful girlfriend makes him feel in control and better about himself.

There is a pattern between Kate's story and my own, both partners are insecure, are too afraid to share their feelings. Instead, they mentally abuse us to make us feel worthless about ourselves so that they can feel better. Maybe you can relate to this?

As you have learned, there are many factors why we self-loathe, once you start questioning yourself and researching your essence, you will finally understand why you hate yourself. This is half the battle, and you are almost there to begin to accept who you are. Many books cover this topic in great detail, I have just briefly browsed over some of the main ones.

Helping Kate, she is now on her path of self-love, growing stronger each day. Kate now realises she does not need this man in her life and is capable of looking after her children. She is currently enrolled in a Mental Health course where she would like to help others who have been in similar positions.

"I have an everyday religion that works for me.
Love yourself first, and everything else falls into line."
Lucille Ball

Spiritual Family

This book talks about your Spiritual Family, you may be asking what is my Spiritual Family? What is the meaning of this? Some of you may already know but may need some clarity. Your Spiritual Family consists of many beautiful light beings walking beside you, helping and guiding you. There are Angels, Guides, loved ones that have passed, ascended masters, such as Jesus, fairies, dragons, animals, arcturians, other advanced intergalactic beings, and many more that we do not know of or yet to meet, walking your path with you. One of their soul purposes is to help you live in higher vibrations instead of the lower. Humans have been enslaved for almost 12,000 years to fear, be manipulated, subjected to violence, controlled, lied to, and led by corrupt leaders.

For thousands of years, we have been at war with dark and light, dark has been shadowing our lives for most of it. Part of this battle is an internal affair with horrible negative thoughts, we tend to punish ourselves and begin to down spiral in a self-loathing manner. As beautiful beings, our thoughts are so powerful that they impact not only on ourselves, but also on our environment and our planet, hence negative attracts negative.

With most people worldwide self-loathing, it is causing a massive effect on our planet, creating floods, storms, volcanoes erupting, etc.

Once you start changing your thought patterns to positive, it will significantly impact you, your lifestyle, and your environment. How do you do this? To begin to love yourself, your Spiritual Family will help and guide you on your beautiful journey. Watch out for the magical synchronicity, as there is no such thing as a coincidence. Your Spiritual Family wants you to be patient with yourself, do not run before you can walk.

True Story: Famous Singer
Even though we have these remarkable souls around us, sometimes you may have a famous popstar popping into your dreams or meditation to give you some advice. At present and in the past, I have a close loved one I love unconditionally, unfortunately, this person likes to paint a dark and cruel picture about me. She has attacked me with her poisonous lies in front of an audience to make me look bad, she has spread venomous lies to family and friends, so their attitude towards me is appalling. I have tried to talk to her about this with love and dignity, but verbal abuse was all I got. "You are insane," "you are deluded," "you have issues," "there is something seriously wrong with you," or "I don't know what you are talking about?" In the past, with my self-loathing consuming me, I took this to heart and internally punished myself with horrible thoughts and self-neglect.

Starting my self-love journey, in my self-care package that I designed myself (we will look at this in later chapters), one of the things I included was to meditate frequently.

One morning while meditating, I could not believe who popped in. Michael Jackson told me to keep my chin up, keep going, not give up, and not be afraid. He knew that I was worried that if my book did well, this person would paint a horrible picture about me to the press, was it worth doing it? Out of all the people in spirit, Michael understood what I was going through. Just looking at his time on earth, he was ridiculed with false allegations, but he never stopped making his music. At the end of the day, with self-love and compassion for oneself, it does not matter what others think of you, it's how you feel about yourself. Me, I think I am a Rockstar!

Thank you, Michael Jackson, for your kind words and wisdom.

Working with your Spiritual Family, you never know who might pop in, it is such a joyous and magical ride. Start today and embrace the beautiful wisdom and guidance of your Spiritual Family.

Always believe in yourself. No matter who is around you being negative or thrusting negative energy at you, totally block it off, because whatever you believe, you become.
Michael Jackson

The Ugly Stick

The Ugly Stick is a term of phrase that Running Bear told me about, it is a powerful mental tool that we beat ourselves up.

Most of us experience forty-eight thousand negatives thoughts per day. We are creatures of habit, and no matter our background, whether it was dark or light, we carry an Ugly Stick. When things go awry, or someone is being negative or failing at something, we automatically pick up our ugly stick and start to beat ourselves.

Some of you may only do this for a few brief moments, whereas some will beat yourself into a mental state of despair. My advice to you whether you only do this for a moment, a day, or weeks is to:

DROP IT DROP IT DROP IT

Somewhere in your life journey, mostly when you are young and vulnerable, you had a negative experience, whether it was a teacher, parent, friend, or family member being mean to you. What they have done is planted seeds into your head. Those horrible, mean, cruel words are still much, very alive in your head today, even though these people may be out of your life, you continue to torture yourself. In my case, those haunting and painful memories that I experienced as a small child conditioned me to think that I was ugly and a horrible being. I felt I deserved all the cruelty that life would bring.

I am telling you; you do not deserve this cruel behaviour or these obnoxious words any more.

Exercise 1 "Fighting Your Inner Demons"

This exercise can help you fight these demons (cruel experiences). Find a quiet place, think of a negative experience in your past, try and go to your earliest memory.

For example: Maybe you came last in a race, and your parent or teacher were disappointed with you. Think of how you felt at that moment. I bet you tried your best, but it was not good enough for them. For a moment, you are the adult addressing the small child (you). What would you say to that little child? Would you scold him/her? Would you be mean to him/her? The answer would be NO, you would not. What kind of words would you say? Speak to them out loud. Shower that small child with love and healing, give him/her a loving hug. You may have to repeat this several times, over a short period, have patience. What you are doing is healing old wounds that have been festering for some time. Maybe in today's life, you may have issues with competition and jealousy that you feel shameful, but you have no idea how to control it. Perhaps in this example, this was the start of you feeling resentful.

There is a pattern of how you are feeling today relating to a past negative experience. Repeat this exercise with other negative experiences, you will get clarity and many realisations. One will undoubtedly be that the blame was not your fault, alleviating the guilt you are holding. You will come to an understanding that these negative people had manipulated you, thinking that you deserved it. When Running Bear told me to do this exercise repeatedly, I had many revelations that helped me forgive myself and let go of guilt and blame. Each time you do this, write in your journal about your self-discoveries.

A note from your Angel

You are beautiful inside and out, your light shines brightly. I know your journey has been challenging, the mistake you have made are your lessons even if you must repeat them many times, I am immensely proud of you.

The Phoenix Moment

How did I start to love myself? It took time as I was so used to beating myself up with my big ugly stick. For a long time, I was reliving my past mistakes.

I kept telling myself that I was a failure, I had two failed marriages, my home repossessed, going bankrupt, a terrible mother, and so on. When I thought I had lost everything, I thought I was worthless, a disappointment – what was the point in carrying on? I had indeed crashed and burned. I was at the lowest point in my life. I had no energy even to contemplate rebuilding.

Running Bear is calling this The Phoenix Moment.

Some of you may have experienced this or going through something like this right now. You feel like you have crashed and burned and do not have the energy to get back on your feet.

A note from Running Bear

When everything burns in flames, and there is nothing left but ash, only then will you rise, you are the Phoenix being reborn.
DROP YOUR UGLY STICK
BE KIND TO YOURSELF

No matter what stage you are in, whether your life is about to go up in flames, or everything around is burning, or the ash is falling.

DROP YOUR UGLY STICK – BE KIND TO YOURSELF
You no longer DESERVE to treat yourself so atrociously.

Exercise 2 "Dear Old Friend"

Many times, I have given out this advice with remarkable results.

Some people seemed it a bit odd at first, some had a deeper understanding of the concept.

It does not matter how you react to this, go with it until you believe this works.

You are naturally a loving soul, a good friend, and a fantastic listener, and you are full of wisdom, helping others (but not yourself), and you freely give your time to help others in despair.

When your dear friend is around at yours crying upon your shoulder, telling you all about her woes, are you cold or unpleasant to her? Do you stamp on her when she is down? No, you do not. You show her kindness, love, and support. From now on, you need to start treating yourself like a dear old friend. When you have a negative thought about yourself, ask yourself, would you say this to your friend? Would you tell her that she was fat, ugly, useless, etc.? When you feel negative about yourself, say some kind, loving words. Speak to yourself in your head or out loud, show yourself some compassion. If you cannot do this, write down in your journal your disturbing thoughts.

Now pretend your friend had written this about herself. Write underneath some thoughtful and nurturing words that you would say to your dear friend, keep repeating this, it does not matter that you are pretending as for one day you will start believing in yourself, start this today.

Just believe in yourself
*   Even if you do not,*
*   pretend that you do and,*
*   as some point, you will*
Venus Williams

Exercise 3 "Your Positives"

I find most people find showing themselves kindness, love, and treating themselves as a dear friend is a hard concept, as they are suffering from low self-esteem and are full of self-loathing. I asked them to name ten positives about themselves, which they all struggle to answer one or two.

When I asked them to name ten negatives, without hesitation, they reel off a long list. I, too, was like this, and I found it hard to say anything positive about me as I clung to my ugly stick. Most of us have at least one loving person in our life that shows us kindness, whether it is a daughter, friend, or spouse. For the first time, do not be afraid to ask for help. Ask them if they could help you make a list of all your positives, you will be pleasantly surprised how people perceive you. When you make your negative list, they will shock you, they will tell you that you do not believe in yourself, you are extremely hard on yourself, and you lack confidence. These comments will be completely different from your negative list, as yours will be cruel and harsh, whereas theirs are not negatives, they are your challenges that you will overcome with time. Write this all down in your journal, and your list will end up looking like this:

My Positives
- I am kind.
- I am caring.
- I am a good mother.
- I am a good wife.
- I am a good friend.
- I have a big loving heart.
- I make excellent cakes and so on.

My Challenges
- To be more confident.
- To love me and put myself first.
- To believe in myself, I do matter.
- To learn how to say No.
- To drop my Ugly Stick and show myself some kindness, and so on.

Have this list where you can see this most days, on your vanity mirror, fridge, or mobile. If you have a moment where you cannot drop your Ugly Stick, pick up your list, and read your positives. Over time, you will start to believe in yourself.

Some of my favourite crystals that will help start your journey to self-love are listed below. See if you can find one for yourself and sit and meditate with it, for a full explanation, please look at chapter "Crystal Healing":

- Black Obsidian – Protection – Healing – Communication
- Black Tourmaline – Protection
- Fluorite – Helps the mind – Grounding – In the now
- Pink Opal – Love – Healing the heart – Releasing old wounds
- Pyrite – Protection – Foresight – Trusting the universe
- Mangano Calcite – Self-love – Healing
- Rose Quartz – Love – Love yourself – Fertility – Healing
- Septarian – Grounding – Patients – Protection

Natural Clearing – Taking Your Power Back

Once you embark on your self-discovery of embracing love for yourself, you will naturally take your power back.

A soul like you tends to give your energy away to your spouse, partners, children, friends, family, and co-workers. You give out your respect, self-worth, confidence, and so much more of yourself to all these people. Some are kind, while others can be cruel and twisted. You intend to please everyone, which is an impossible task, as you always get someone who is ungrateful and demands more of you. Therefore, you take it personally, you feel hurt, incompetent, tired, and worthless. These draining emotions fuel up the self-loathing fire within you. Picking up the ugly stick, you start to beat yourself up; you now become your own worst enemy, in a downward spiral of self-loathing.

STOP STOP STOP STOP...

Exercise 4 "YOU!"
Find a peaceful spot, your bedroom, garden, or sitting in your car.

Take a deep breath in and exhale slowly, do this twice more. Just for a moment, bring your attention to your breathing, it may seem bizarre at first. At this moment, ask yourself, what makes you happy? What are your passions? What is your dream? What would you like to do? Maybe at first, you do not know that all you want is to be happy and feel peace and harmony. If you are finding difficulties, confide in a good friend who will listen and support you.

Get them to help you write in your journal a little to-do list. Once you have completed it, make sure you check it off your list and note how it made you feel. It does not have to be a long sentence, just one or two words will do.

- Get my hair cut – I look so much better.
- Go for a massage – I feel so relaxed.
- Go for a walk in the forest – I felt free.
- Sit by the beach – I love watching the waves, I felt peaceful.
- Have a relaxing bath – I can feel all my tension and stress evaporating.

The aim is to change the way you think, stop beating yourself up, and bring attention to your true self. Use this little exercise every time you start to self-loath.

As mentioned earlier, unfortunately, there are negative people in our lives that significantly challenge us. As a natural giver and people pleaser, these people take advantage of your good nature.

They are used to you saying "Yes" all the time.

There may be times when you are afraid or have no energy to fight to say the word "No."

You watch them throw their toys out the pram, stamping their feet, and causing such a commotion that you give in.

I have come across many people in this situation where they tell me it is simpler to give in.

Exercise 5 "No"
Another little exercise to help those who always give in, is to

practice in front of a mirror, if you are uncomfortable with that, find a quiet little place, bedroom, garden, and practice saying "No" out loud.

Believe it or not, this little word changes the vibrations in your aura, making you feel more energetic, worthy, and you do matter.

They do not know that the word "No" has so much power when you stand by it.

The very first time you use the word "No" is somewhat nerve-racking.

Just believe in you. If you do not want to do something, i.e., give someone a lift, look after a child, do someone's work, say "NO!" The response can vary if they are not used to you saying "No." They are likely to be shocked.

Some may try to emotionally blackmail.

Ask yourself, do you want to do it? You have a choice, and it is okay to say, "No, not today."

When you say your first no, it becomes very empowering, and you realise that you do not deserve to be treated like a mug, fool, etc. It opens your eyes to who is around you, and you start to assess the people around you who are negative and taking advantage of you.

Keep saying "No" to the things you do not want to do and stand by it. The people who threw tantrums will quickly realise that they will not get what they want from you and may leave.

Write down in your journal every time you said "No" to a situation you usually do, how did this make you feel?

True Story: Emma
Emma, a loving, kind soul, had a so-called friend with a child of six years old. Her friend could not take him to school as she never had a car, even though it was a twenty minute walk, she could

not be bothered. She asked Emma if she could get a lift to take them both to school and back. Emma was a bit reluctant at first, but her friend played on her heartstrings. For two years, Emma did the school run even though her children were all grown up, her friend never offered her any petrol money during that time. Then one day, Emma told her she could not do it as she was not feeling well. Her friend was furious and gave her lots of abuse, then stopped speaking to her. Emma felt hurt and used as she found out her so-called friend had found someone else to take them and gave them petrol money.

I asked Emma if she would do this again?

"NO!" she replied.

Saying "No" you are taking your power back, raising your vibration, your self-esteem, self-respect, self-worth, and self-love.

You will then naturally gravitate to positive and loving people, and your tolerance will shorten for those who are hostile towards you. You realise and accept you do not deserve to be oppressed.

Over time, continuing to say "No" when you want to, you naturally start to cleanse your life. Friends and co-workers may be a natural phase, but when it comes to spouses, partners, and family, this can be the most difficult challenge. I am not going to lie, but the people we love the most are the ones that hurt us the most.

I have had two abusive marriages and divorcing both husbands was challenging, but it became the best thing I ever did for myself. The most formidable challenge and the most hurtful one is when it comes to our children. As parents, we love our children unconditionally, but when they grow up and become cruel and abusive towards you, what do you do?

True story: A Child of Mine

For years I battled with one of my children, tried, and tried to get her help, she would not except mine. For years I beat myself up, wondering what I had done wrong? Blaming myself for her cruel, abusive behaviour, at times, I was at fault for lashing out at her, as I could not cope with her response. On many occasions, I tried to talk to her to no avail. She has now completely shut me out of her life. She sees me as a failure, a rubbish mum of five children, losing the family home, two failed marriages, suffering from depression, a woman having to go bankrupt, and now penniless and worthless. In her eyes, I am nothing, and for many years I believed she was right. Now, I know that I am a good person, a loving mother, I have tried my best, and yes, I have made mistakes along the way. But all these failures are my valuable lessons that have allowed me to evolve into this beautiful light being today, and you too can develop. If you are experiencing anything like this, you will know this is the most heart-breaking situation. Remember, you do not deserve to be treated in this way, no matter your past mistakes. Take some simple steps, start saying "I love me" out loud, and let these healing words radiate through your aura.

Even though I am out of her life, and I do think it is best for now. There is not a day that I do not think about her and my grandchildren. I send her love and healing, and I hope maybe one day we can reunite.

Taking back my power by saying "No" even though it has been challenging, my mental health has improved significantly; I have claimed back my self-respect, self-worth, my confidence has grown, and I know now that I am a lovely human being. I am no longer afraid to say NO when I want to.

Start today and start practice saying NO and claim back your power. The more you stand by your "No" the healthier you will become, which will allow the universe to open its doors of opportunities to you.

A note from your Angel
Only do things you love and stop saying, yes, when you do not mean it.

Learn to say "No" without feeling guilty as this is teaching you to learn how to respect and take care of yourself.

Some of my favourite crystals that will help take your power back, see if you can find one for yourself and sit and meditate with it, for a full explanation, please look at chapter "Crystal Healing":

• Blue Goldstone – Confidence – Opportunities – Stand in your power – Healing

• Chevron Amethyst – Spiritual – Protection – Best version of yourself – Strength

• Dendritic Agate – Peace – Confidence – Protection – Abundance – Prosperity

• Fluorite – Helps the mind – Grounding – In the now

• Morganite – New love – Healing heart

Change Your Reaction

While you are naturally going through a clearing, gravitating to more positive people, and spending less time with negative energy, it can be difficult living with undesirable families, partners/spouses, children.

Unfortunately, I do not have a magic wand, so I cannot change their bad behaviour towards you, I wish, but I can give you some simple tools to use. We cannot change anyone, but we can change the way we react – the first tool in your belt, as mentioned in the earlier chapter. Saying "no" and telling yourself daily, "I love me." These words are very empowering and healing.

Some of you may think if you are in a negative situation with someone, simply leave. That is brilliant if that is an option, whereas some feel an element of entrapment and isolation.

Some relationships are dependent on finances, maybe they cannot afford to part, some are dependent on the child, they could not cope on their own, some are dependant as they are too afraid to be on their own. There are many other reasons for staying in a negative situation.

For whatever reason you may be in an unhealthy situation, feeling lost, sad, and hopeless, starting this self-love journey will change all of this, but first, while in this situation, you need to start changing the way you react. Changing the way you react is another way to claim your power back, and I am telling you it works. I have known women and men who were miserable and suffered from their nerves, self-confidence, self-loathing, etc. that have turned their lives around, are happy and have a more fulfilled life, but most importantly, they love themselves.

True Story: Susan
Susan's husband came home from work one evening, where she had cooked him his favourite steak and homemade chips.

She placed it on the dining table in front of him. She noticed that he was in a dark mood and was grateful the children were all upstairs playing in their bedrooms. As soon as the plate of food was placed in front of him, he exploded.

He was vial, cruel, and abusive towards her, shouting that what she had served up was disgusting. Susan felt awful that she had got it so wrong, he made her feel worthless and unworthy of him.

Susan quickly grabbed the plate and hurried off to the kitchen to cook him something else, feeling awful about herself.

This was not a one-off, whatever Susan did for him, he would make her feel incompetent and useless and that she was lucky to have him. At the time, she felt trapped, Susan feared to be on her own with her children. How would she cope? Susan had no money; she did not want to ask for help from friends or family. Susan did not want to impose her burdens upon them. If she did leave him, Susan was petrified she would spend the rest of her life on her own, who would want her?

How would you advise Susan?

What do you think Susan should do differently?

How do you think Susan should react to her husband's outbursts?

It turns out that Susan is a good cook, whatever she makes is always tasty as I have experienced first-hand, but it did not matter in this situation. It was a lack of respect, and the way he treated her was the problem. After chatting with Susan and telling her I could not transplant a new personality into him, it had to come within. She needed to help herself. I told her to be brave and change her reaction.

The next time it happened, which was not long after the last episode, again, he exploded and took everything out on Susan. She intuitively knew there was nothing wrong with the meal, there was nothing wrong with her. Susan realised that she did not deserve to be treated in this way. So, she told him from now on to cook his own meal and left the room. She claimed her power back and felt accelerated with joy.

Her husband was left speechless and later grovelled to her. Over time with her confidence growing and reclaiming her power, Susan realised that she did not deserve this ill-treatment, she started her self-love journey. Susan is now happily living on her own with her children.

A note from Running Bear

You cannot change people's behaviour towards you,

You have the power within to change your reaction to their behaviour.

Remember, these people are powerless without your reaction.

Here are some of my favourite crystals that will help you change your reaction, see if you can find one for yourself and sit and meditate with it. For a full explanation, please look at chapter "Crystal Healing":

- Black Obsidian – Protection – Healing – Communication
- Black Tourmaline – Protection

- Dendritic Agate – Peace – Confidence – Protection – Abundance – Prosperity
- Fluorite – Helps the mind – Grounding – In the now
- Pyrite – Protection – Foresight – Trusting the universe
- Septarian – Grounding – Patients – Protection

Givers & Takers

There are many different types of people, but the most popular types are Givers or Takers, another way to look at it is Warm or Cold People. We all know these types of people who are in our lives today. Many of you that are reading this are Givers.

You have big hearts, and you give so much of your energy, time, love, money, etc. to others. You have been doing this for years and years that you have completely lost yourself. When was the last time you did something for yourself? Your dreams, hobbies, etc. forgotten about. You have sacrificed yourself for others.

Being a mother or father, we are devoted to giving our children the best and safe upbringing, again, we tend to naturally fall into the trap of giving too much. I have known mothers to overcompensate with their time, money, love, due to a marriage break up. I have known fathers to shed with all their money, buying their children presents, etc. hoping that they will love them more.

For example, when I divorced my first husband, I was left to raise our five children single-handed. My husband was not consistent with spending time with them, he would probably make time for them about five times a year. My heart broke for my children. I tried to reason with my ex, practically begging him to see his children to no avail, and received a lot of abuse from him. I felt a failure, I felt guilty, I felt anger, I felt a lot of horrible things, but most of all, I thought I had let my children down.

My mother accused me of spoiling my children, I knew I was overcompensating, showering them with holidays, presents, etc. I felt I had to make up for their absent father. This Giver behaviour pattern that I had learned at a young age, wanting to please people, I applied this to all my relationships, friends, boyfriends, family, etc. I gave too much that I had completely forgotten about me.

How many of you have done the same?

I bet most of you who are reading this can relate.

True Story: Florida

In my first marriage, I had surrendered myself to my children and husband, everything I did was for them.

My husband told me he wanted to go to Florida to Disneyland, and some of his friends would like to come as well. He said to me to organised and provide an itinerary plan, as all I do is stay home and look after the children, according to him I did not work. There were twelve of us, including our children, I had to get tickets, flights, accommodation, car, and sort out the money into dollars for everyone.

I was frightened; I have never been given such a responsible task, I knew if I got anything wrong, my husband would sure point it out, making me feel awful. I was so focused on the job, not forgetting anyone's needs. I even had to provide a list of items and clothing to the other couples, so they knew what they needed to pack. I was nervous and paranoid that I was going to forget something. I did not want to let anyone down (people-pleasing). I made my list of everything, researching the best way to get the most out of our Disney tickets and providing a two-week itinerary.

Finally, when we all arrived in Florida, we had a lovely Villa. I was unpacking the children's and my husband's clothes, checking my list. I was incredibly pleased with myself that I had not forgotten anything. It was not until I went to unpack my case. OMG! I had forgotten most of my clothes. All I had was my underwear and swimwear.

This was a huge realisation; I had been so worried about taking care of everyone else's needs that I had forgotten about myself. This is what happens to people who give and give, they forget about themselves, their vocabulary consists of Yes and Sorry.

How many of you say "Sorry" all the time?

My beautiful guide Running Bear has been working with me, I can now proudly say the word "No" within that, I have reclaimed most of my power back. I am still on my journey to Self-Love, and life presents many challenges, and one of them is to stop saying sorry for things that I have no control over.

Exercise 6 "Sorry"

Try for one day, count how many times you say the word "Sorry." Write down in a journal what prompted you to say it.

Have two columns, was it in your control or out of your control. If you made a mistake, i.e., Put sugar in your friend's tea when they do not have sugar, that would be in your control, hence it is a valid "Sorry." Out of your control, i.e., your partner has misplaced his razor and accuses you of taking it. This is not the case, but you are full of apologies and help him to find it.

He finds it and remembers that he did place it in a different location. You are feeling relieved, but how many "Sorrys" did you say?

Control Sorry	Qty	Out of your Control Sorry	Qty
Sugar in friend's tea	1	misplace razor blamed me	7

Writing in your journal will provide you with clarity. When you start to ask yourself questions, you will open your eyes, sparking many revelations.

Why do you have to be sorry if he misplaced his razor?

You know you never touch it, why did you say sorry for something you never did?

Why are you sorry for his bad behaviour towards you?

Keep updating your journal, and in time the column 'Out of your Control Sorry' will vanish.

As mentioned before in the earlier chapter, saying the word "NO" has so much strength in it, as you are taking your power back.

True Story: No
At first, saying, No was an impossible task for me.

I was the person who would willingly give details to strangers on the street who were stopping passers-by for all different reasons. I would give out my bank details to adopt a child in Africa, save the whales, children's hospitals, dog homes, etc. I could not afford it, but I could not refuse them. Once I got home, I would cancel it all, but I could not say no to their faces.

How many of you change your electric and gas supplier? When cold callers came knocking on my door and offer me cheaper rates, I could not say No. Over the years, I had so many different suppliers. I even invited the well-dressed people into my home that preached about their religion, offering them tea and biscuits. I was accused by friends that I was too soft.

Maybe so, all I do know saying "Yes" all the time can bring a lot of trouble and a lot of pain. No matter how much you give, you cannot please them all.

Running Bear has taught me, and yes, it took a while for me to accept it, that the only person you should please is yourself.

Stress, anxiety, and depression are caused when we are living to please others.

Paulo Coelho

Pleasing myself and saying the word "NO" was initially a selfish concept for me, but once I accepted and started to practice, I felt my whole being growing, shedding of the dark heavy, gloomy cloak surrounding me. My self-worth, my self-respect, my self love bloomed as I came into my true self. I took back my power that I freely gave to others, now I say, 'no thank you' to the cold callers on the street, and at my door.

I can say, 'no, this is not for me' to the religious people knocking on my door. I feel no guilt, no shame, I feel proud to be myself. This will happen for you, too, when you start your Self-Love journey.

It is okay to say No, start today. Maybe you do not want to go out with your friend, or give someone a lift, or watch a boring programme on the TV, or work overtime, or give away your last £10. Again, asked yourself do you want to do it? Do you have the time, energy, or resources? What would you like to do instead? Relax in the bath? Have a cuppa? Watch your favourite programme on TV?

Practice out loud the word NO, reap the benefits from it. At first, saying No is daunting, there may be people who will react surprised at No. They might act up, so you will give in to Yes.

Stand firm, keep to a No, and if you do buckle, you have not failed.

Write down in your journal of how it made you feel. Write down what you would have done instead if you had said No. What would you have like to do, instead? Write a list of all the things you could have done.

Maybe the top of your list was nothing.

That is okay. Nothing is essential as it is your time with yourself.

A note from your Angel

You are a beautiful, brave, loving being, keep on practising the word "NO."

Keep focusing on yourself and spend your time, energy, and conversation around people who inspire, support, and help you.

Some of my favourite crystals that will help take care of yourself and better your relationships are listed below. See if you can find one for yourself and sit and meditate with it, for a full explanation, please look at chapter "Crystal Healing":

- Angelite – Angels – Spirit – Protection – Spiritual Growth
- Aura Rose Quartz – Romance – Love for yourself – Finding yourself
- Lapis lazuli – Healing headaches – Spiritual enlightenment – Improving relationships
- Mangano Calcite – Self-love – Healing
- Pink Opal – Love – Healing the heart – Releasing old wounds
- Rose Quartz – Love – Love yourself – Fertility – Healing

The Sealion – The Shark –
The Dolphin

As mentioned before there are different kinds of people in the world, I have spoken about Givers who give most of their time and energy to others, leaving themselves broken, distraught, and unhappy with their lives. The takers with their narcissistic attitude, will endlessly take and take to purely satisfy their own needs, which can be endless.

Running Bear showed me in a meditation of such people in a metaphoric way. He showed me a Sealion sitting on a small floating iceberg with lots of fish surrounding her. Each fish representing a part of the sealion:

 ➢ Love
 ➢ Kindness
 ➢ Respect
 ➢ Self-Worth
 ➢ Confidence
 ➢ Happiness
 ➢ Yes / Sorry
 ➢ Dreams etc

He then showed me a Shark circling the Sealion, he had nothing but hunger going through his mind.

The Sealion was afraid of the shark but felt sorry for it as she knew it was hungry, so the Sealion threw it a fish (self-respect). The Shark shredded it to pieces and devoured every bit. The Sealion felt pleased, she was helping the Shark and continued to keep throwing him a fish. No matter how much the Sealion fed the Shark, the Sealion could not satisfy the Shark's hunger, eventually, there were no more fish to feed him. All the Sealion had left was herself. What should the Sealion do?

It was in her nature to give, should she sacrifice herself to please the Shark?

How many of you have sacrificed everything for someone whose temperaments are like the Shark?

How many of you have a Shark in your lives now?

During this meditation, I asked Running Bear, don't Sealion eat fish? He replied, we can be our own worst enemy devouring and slowly destroying ourselves.

So, who are you, a Sealion or Shark?

A Sealion who devours themselves and feeds the Shark?

Once you become aware of who you are and the people in your lives, this is a transformative moment that will enable you to slowly evolve into a beautiful Dolphin.

The Dolphin is happy, a free spirit to explore new wonders and possibilities, throws caution to the wind, and is free of fears and worries. The Dolphin has the strength to scare off any Sharks by swimming at speed with its power. The Dolphin has a healthy balance of being able to say "Yes" and "No".

The dolphin shines with confidence, aspiration, and self-love. Dolphins are nurturing and have been known to help and look after different species without judgment of discrimination. Once you become aware of who you are and the people in your lives, this is a transformative moment that will enable you to slowly evolve into a beautiful Dolphin.

If you are a Shark, you can evolve also, regardless of age, gender, culture or what you have done in the past.

True Story: John

I know a man in his late sixties, his whole life he had been a predator, a Shark. Taking and destroying people's lives, he enjoyed inflicting pain upon others. Then one day out of the blue, he did not like the person he had become. He knew he could not change his past, but he no longer wanted to be this dark creature. He wanted to change, to evolve, he started to give back. Working as a builder he never charged his customers, working for free. He had thousands of pounds in his bank account which he acquired over the years by taking, he gave to charity. He bought a rescued a dog (which was unusual as he did not like animals) and gave him a loving home, this dog has taught him so much about love. With these small changes, it has transformed him into a beautiful Dolphin, helping and nurturing others.

It does not matter where you start, Sealion or Shark, you can grow and evolve into a beautiful Dolphin.

Thank you, Running Bear, for sharing this with us.

The World Today

Back in the Victorian times, a plump lady seemed to be attractive as she was associated with wealth, whereas a slim lady was deemed a wench and associated with poverty.

Even if a rich lady were slim, she would be dressed to make herself larger. In today's time, with social media dominating the world, being a size zero for a woman is now associated with being attractive. Being a plump woman, such as me, I have been judged as morbidly obese. I can tell you when you have been called the latter, and in a dark mindset of self-loathing, this is soul-destroying to hear. There are health complications of being overweight, but there are also health implications for those who strive to be a perfect size. This does not only affect women, but men are also under tremendous pressure to look a specific size and shape, taking harmful drugs to achieve their goals. Both sexes are more body-conscious, getting surgery, peck, and boob implants, and both having Botox and Fillers. Permanent makeup tattooed on their faces; it is endless. No one wants to age as they are afraid of losing their looks, whereas one fifty years ago to age was a gift, as most people died before they were forty.

I have found most people of today are brainwashed, it's everywhere, magazines, billboards, adverts, social media, TV reality shows, telling us to look in a precise way to be beautiful, but all we are doing is learning how to look at ourselves with critical eyes as well as judging others.

True Story: "You are Fat"

When I was in my thirties, I was raising my five children single-handedly, and doing a full-time degree course, which had its stresses and pressures. So, every two weeks I looked forwards to going out with some of my friends.

Sometimes we would go for a meal or out for a few drinks. I had a friend who always came out with me, she was only a few years older than me, she was tall, blonde, and slim. At the time, I was blonde and plump build. Her comments were a bit harsh, she would often tell me, "You are fat." I would ignore her or laugh it off. We were both single, when we went out, she loved the attention of men. She would tell me the handsome man talking to us was hers and that I did not stand a chance with him. "Look at you, look at me." I know what you are thinking, this friend was not a real friend to me, but at the time, I did not love myself. In today's time, if someone treated me like this, I would not tolerate this behaviour. Anyway, getting back to the story. The handsome man in question, my friend, was all over him, but he turned down her advances and ended up asking me out on a date. You can imagine her reaction, she was furious. Sadly, for her, this happened on most occasions. She was confused. "I don't understand it, why are they going for you?" She looked at me in disgust. "When they can have me."

Eventually, over time her behaviour got worse, she became aggressive and violent to men who were only interested in me. She became more abusive towards me, things got bad that I had to end our relationship. Looking back, she was brainwashed, with her plastic boobs, Fillers, Botox, and slim body, she thought she was the body of beauty.

A few years later, I found a scientific study about men's preferences, that the majority of men preferred the plump woman shape. I call it the natural woman shape, and most women preferred a tummy on their men.

Whatever size, colour, shape, or gender you are, all the imperfections you see make you unique and special.

My boobs do not sit where they use to be, my tummy no longer flat. Loving yourself, you embrace it all and no longer care about the mole, or sagging skin, scars, stretch marks etc. Start today and take off your critical glasses and start seeing the beauty in yourself and others.

Start cherishing your body and tell yourself you are beautiful. Appreciating yourself for who you are and what you have, you will realise your true worth. You will not settle for anything less.

A note from your Angel
You are special and unique, embrace the things with love that you think is ugly, i.e., wrinkles, being plump, too skinny, wonky toes, scars, etc. Remember, there is no other you in this world, loving yourself is the key to your happiness.

I think we should be taught at an early age how to love ourselves; it should be compulsory in school, part of the curriculum. This could prevent a lot of pain, anxiety, and depression, which is on the rise.

Mental Health in our society is a significant problem, it has been reported one out of three people will suffer in their lifetime.

Being bullied is a horrible and traumatic experience. We automatically think of the word bully and get transported back to the school playground. However, this is not the case, bullies are everywhere, and age does not matter. It can come in all manners and cred, work, friends, family, but most alarming is the internet.

With technology taking over, bullying is increasing, with cyberbullying and trolling, suicides in teenagers have dramatically increased.

Being a teenager is possibly the worst time of your life, your hormones are all over the place, your body transforming, enhancing your insecurities.

There are young girls and boys getting Botox, Fillers, Nose, and Boob jobs, etc. Social media such as Facebook, Instagram, Snapchat, etc., have made it easy for trolls to target anyone that does not fit in their perfect mould. If you are in this horrible position or know of anyone, they are picking on you because you are unique and are jealous of your light. Do not let them win, send healing to the troll, and ask for healing and protection from your Spiritual Family.

Follow these exercises within this book, write in your journal, talk to your Guide and your Angels, who stand beside you, who are always willing to help you. Ask them for their guidance and watch out for the miracle that they will perform. Remember, you are never on your own.

Let us go back twenty, thirty, forty years, if you heard anyone saying they loved themselves, they would be immediately judged as egotistic and full of themselves, big-headed, even selfish. This stigma still stands today.

Even if you come from a loving family, parents adoring you, giving you a fantastic childhood. Sadly, your parents cannot protect you all the time. I have known people who have come to me for a reading who have had these loving beings in their life suffering from anxiety, low self-esteem, lack of confidence, hating themselves due to a negative experience from the past.

Horrible bullies, negative people, that is all it takes, one nasty comment to trigger you into a self-hating spiral.

You can end this vicious circle of self-loathing by starting your self-love journey, you will then be able to help your family and friends to start theirs. Once they are on their quest, they will be inspired to help others. Just imagine this beautiful ripple effect impacting the world with love. Imagine, over generations, this world will be such a joyous place to live.

A note from Running Bear

Your thoughts and actions, you think they are like stones, just dropped into the ocean.

Just look at the ripple effect one drop can make.

One small positive change can have an enormous impact on a person's life, their family, and their environment.

Loneliness

We are born alone, we live alone, we die alone. Only through our love and friendship can we create the illusion for the moment that we are not alone.
Orson Welles

I would like to say Orson Welles quote is correct in the physical sense, but spiritually, this is not true. We are never alone, as we are surrounded by our beautiful Spiritual Family. Yes, we have all felt lonely somewhen in our lives, and it can be when we are surrounded by our loved ones, i.e., partner, children, family members, and friends. In my first marriage raising my children, I have never felt so alone.

True Story: The Deal

I was in my late twenties, the children were all so young, and I lived in an abusive relationship that had started to take its toll on me. My husband hated his children and resented me for having them, he did not want anything to do with them. When he got home in the evenings from work, I made sure that they were all fed, bathed, and put to bed. The house would be spotless, with a home-cooked meal waiting for him.

Anything out of place, and he would be even more of a nightmare. Every evening I would be on tender-hooks, hoping and praying that the children would not wake up as he screamed verbal abuse at me. He demanded that I ought to kiss his feet, he thought he was a god.

I tried to reason with him but to no avail. I could not confide in anyone; he would always scare people away. Feeling alone and isolated, I started to feel trapped and extremely unhappy with my life.

I hated going to bed, knowing full well that I would wake up beside him. It was becoming evident that I no longer wanted to wake up. I could not face another day with him, and the only way out of this hell pit was to kill myself.

On Thursday evening, when he got home from work, the children were all tucked up in bed fast asleep. I found it extremely hard tucking them into bed and reading their favourite story. It would be the last time I would see their perfect angelic faces. I sat on the sofa waiting for the front door to open, I could not wait to go. I did not have to wait long. He stormed through the house to the kitchen. He realised that I had not cooked his dinner, he was furious with me, but I did not care. My mind was elsewhere. I had already packed a piece of hosepipe and a towel and put them in the boot of the car, I could not wait to be free.

I grabbed my car keys and fled for the door. For a split second, I thought he would stop me, I rarely ventured out in the evening.

Wouldn't he be curious where I was going? I was wrong. He stood and stared hard at me, giving me an icy cold stare that sent shivers up my spine.

I parked in a dark, quiet car park surrounded by trees, I thought it would give me some privacy.

I positioned the car near to the trees in the far corner of the car park.

Getting out of the car, I placed the hose pipe firmly into the exhaust pipe and carefully putting the other end into the back-passenger window. I constantly kept looking over my shoulder, making sure no one was around, the thought of someone trying to stop me was terrifying. Using the towel, I blocked the little gap at the top of the window.

Getting back into the car, I locked all the doors, there was no hesitation in my actions. I placed my trembling fingers onto the keys, I was ready to ignite the engine.

Suddenly a police car pulled into the car park, and my heart jumped. What if they saw the pipe? They parked in front of me, their bright beams lit up my car. I held my breath as I frantically tried to come up with an excuse. They sat in front of me for only a few moments, which seemed forever. I let a sigh of relief as they turned around and exited the car park. Phew!

I thought they had discovered what I was planning.

As I sat there trying to breathe, a wave of guilt consumed me.

I could not leave this world without leaving a message for my children. Pulling a piece of paper and pen out of the glove compartment, I stared blankly at it. What was I going to say to them? How can I explain my selfish act? I loved my children; they were my world. How could I leave them? How could I leave them with him? I felt tears rolling down my cheeks, the conflicting thoughts were tearing up my mind. I cannot do this. I cannot go on. My life had become hell. I cannot take any more. Chucking the paper and pen to one side, I decided there was no way to justify my actions, I was a poor excuse for a mother. Placing my fingers around the keys, I went to turn them.

"Maxine, don't!" A voice bellowed out.

I jumped out of my skin but looking around, I could not see anyone. Shaking it off and thinking it was my imagination, I continued with my actions.

"Maxine! Stop!"

I instantly recognised the voice.

"Dad?"

"Yes! Don't do it!" he pleaded.

Glancing beside me, there was no one sitting there, but I knew he was right beside me; it was weird hearing him so clearly.

"Dad, you don't understand," I cried.

"Yes, I do, I know it's been hard…"

"Hard? Hard is an understatement… Dad… I do not have the strength to go on… I cannot go on… I just can't!"

"Maxine, please don't do this… I promise you… I promise you things will change!"

"Change, how can it change? There is no change, it is just going to get worse and worse… I just want out." My fingers twitched around the keys.

"Maxine, just listen to me… I promise you things will change… in three weeks, things will be different."

I could not help but laugh out loud at the absurd statement. I wiped the tears from my face.

"How?" I was sceptical.

"Trust me," he reasoned.

For the next two hours, I argued with Dad. He would not tell me how things would change.

"Trust me, I promise you, I will always be by your side," was the only information he would give me.

Finally, I agreed to his terms – that I would wait for three weeks, but I promised him if nothing had changed, I would return, and then nothing would stop me.

Going home to Reece, I was filled up with mixed emotions. A part of me was angry that I had agreed to Dad's deal. Another aspect of me was anxious and worried as to how I would survive the next three weeks. I have never felt so tired, so beaten and so worn out. What was in store for me? Why couldn't he just let me go? As I slumped into the armchair, Reece was like an angry rattlesnake waiting to kill its prey. He had seen from my swollen eyelids that I had been crying. I looked distraught and tired, Reece was in his element – seeing me so weak, he thrived. For the next hour, Reece took great delight tearing me to shreds.

Reece was the only person I confided in. At the beginning of the relationship, when I was fourteen, I told him my dark secrets of being raped multiple times, beaten, abused, etc. He told me to shut my mouth and never to mention it again. He was evil with his words, bringing up the horrific events and twisting the truth in a malicious venomous way. He made me feel sick. How can someone twist something so terrible to make that person feel worse? What sort of person is that? Sadly, this was not the first occasion he had brought my traumatic past up. I wished I had never told him. I felt my self-sinking, I was drowning, and I had never felt so alone.

Tears poured down my face. Why me?

What had I done so wrong to be mistreated? Was it because I was so horrible? Or was it a combination of things? I knew I was a terrible mother; I knew that I was fat and ugly, I should be grateful, he was a good-looking man. Without him, I was worthless, I would not be able to cope. I knew I could not do better than him. Tears poured down my face... all the horrible things he said... he was right. Seeing me so vulnerable, he could not help himself, he placed his face into mine and laughed at me. He told me I was weak and stupid.

Suddenly I felt a warm, loving, invisible blanket had been placed around my shoulders, this strange and wonderful sensation stopped my tears and feelings of despair.

I was in a world of my own, ignoring his abusive comments, which seemed to bounce off my protective blanket. I stared at the raving, ranting, mad man, I did not know him any more. Feelings I had for him seemed to evaporate from my being.

His cruel words no longer had any effect. Calmly and coldly, I stood up and looked fearlessly into his eyes. He was startled by my bizarre behaviour, which rendered him speechless.

"Goodnight!" I walked out of the room and headed for the bedroom.

I do not know what happened that night, maybe it was Dad protecting me, but whatever it was, that loving, warm blanket hugged me tightly for the next three weeks.

Reece's abusive behaviour went through the roof, he tried everything to get a response out of me, but it did not matter what he did, he just could not get through.

Three weeks to the day, I had to drop my car off at the garage, it was due to have new brake pads. My mum popped round to look after the younger children while I dropped the car off. I had arranged with Reece for him to pick me up from the garage. I knew he resented doing me a favour, but I just did not care what he thought.

It was just after eleven o'clock in the morning, and I was waiting outside the garage. Reece promised me his meeting would be over in time to collect me. Suddenly I heard a car beep. I looked across the street, and Reece was waving excitedly.

"Quick, get in!"

I jumped into the car, and Reece quickly found a car parking space, he could not contain his excitement, he kept jumping up and down in his seat.

"Maxine! Guess what? I've got some brilliant news!"

I stared coldly at him. I could not care less if he had just won the lottery.

"What?" I was cold as ice.

"I've got a job promotion!" He bounced up and down.

"Good for you," I said flatly.

"You know what that means? More money!" he yelped.

"Great!" I was not enthused.

"But there is one thing though!" he added caution to his tone.

"What?" I was getting bored.

"It all depends on you?"

"Me? Why me?" I was so disinterested.

"Well, it means… I will have to work away every week and come home at weekends… but I might have to work weekends to start with," he said hesitantly.

Suddenly I felt my ears prick up. Did I hear right? Did it mean that I did not have to wake up to him every day and be subjected to his abuse?

I felt a huge weight lift from my shoulders, suddenly, I could see the light. A big smile beamed across my face, this was the best news ever, it was better than winning the lottery.

"When do you start?" I asked all excitedly.

He gritted his teeth, oh no, I thought, it is going to be months away.

"I start next week… is that okay?"

I could not contain myself. I screamed out in excitement. The silly man rejoiced with me, too, obviously for a different reason.

"Look, this will be a temporary measure… once I am established, maybe in six months or so, we could sell the house and have you and the kids move nearer. That way, we can all be together," he tried to reassure me.

You must be kidding, I thought to myself. I knew for sure I would not sell the house to move nearer to him, I knew that I could make this a permanent measure, and I did – a year after this arrangement, I finally found the courage and divorced him.

I would like to say a big thank you to my dad for throwing me a lifeline when I needed it.

Love you always, Dad.

Loneliness with self-loathing is a killer, all we have to do is look at the celebrities that we think have it all: fame, success, money, Oscars, Grammy awards, etc., who tragically end up killing themselves.

It does not matter who you are, whether you are someone living on the streets to someone living in a castle, loneliness affects everyone at some point in our lives, and combining it with self-loathing is toxic for our souls.

Just remember you are never on your own. Look out for the signs, talk to your Spiritual Family, ask them for their help. Feel their touch holding onto your hand, with your inner voice telling you things will be okay, this is them. Write down your dreams in your journal, your Spiritual Family loves to communicate with you in this way. It may not resonate at the time, but when the time is right, usually when we feel lonely, it will lift your spirits and prove they are always there for you. As you sit by yourself in your little room feeling sad, your room is full to the brim with your Spiritual Family.

Loving yourself, you will invite beautiful Spiritual magic into your lives, you will never feel lonely or unlove again.

A note from your Angel
Remember, dear one, I am standing right beside you and ready to help and comfort you whenever you ask.

Breathe deeply, take each day as it comes, and remember

that tomorrow is another day where anything is possible.

Here are some of my favourite crystals that will help you with loneliness and gaining your power back. See if you can find one for yourself and sit and meditate with it, for a full explanation, please look at chapter "Crystal Healing":
- Amethyst – Tranquillity – Spiritual wisdom – Protection
- Aquamarine – Healing – Courage – Judgmentalism
- Mangano Calcite – Self-love – Healing
- Rose Quartz – Love – Love yourself – Fertility – Healing
- Sodalite – Spiritual Growth – Believe in yourself – Helps grief

The Now

Many of us blunder through life with lots of negative things happening repeatedly. Living hell on a repetitive loop. Some of us have no direction, some of us have no clue, and some have plans that have failed. Some of us have adopted an attitude that life is not fair, which I have been guilty of.

We tend to be caught up either in the Past or Future, we forget about the Now.

Now is the most essential time. Anxiety is associated with our future, and Depression is linked to the past. Now, can have a significant change in how we view everything. Acceptance is key to our self-love journey. Once we accept, yes, bad things have happened, we cannot change the past, Now, you can breathe, even pause for a moment, even if times are hard right now.

When you look back at your past, ask yourself, what lessons have you learned? Pain and Love are both of our most outstanding teachers. There were probably periods of darkness in your past that you eventually overcame. This shows strength and wisdom, you may have discovered your intuition, that gut feeling you had was always right. It may have taken you down a few dark paths to believe in yourself.

For example, when I first met my first and second husband. My intuition, my gut, told me these men were not good. Back then, I did not believe in myself and ignored these warnings.

Consequently, I learned many painful lessons with each one of them. I questioned myself, "why me?" I thought life was unfair as I endured many painful traumas. For several years I suffered from severe depression, continually wanting to end my life.

I isolated myself away from family and friends, the only companion I had was my beautiful cat. Being in the Now, I can see my pain and my lessons. I am now more energetic; I am wiser; I have evolved. I listen to my intuition – gut feeling, as it always steers me right, and I have established an excellent relationship with my guide, Running Bear. How did I do this? I accepted that I could not change my past, living in the NOW and appreciating everything I have. I lost the big five-bedroom house, the hot tub, the brand-new car, and the so-called friends and horrible husbands. I now live in a tiny flat on my own. I have a second-hand car that never lets me down, I am surrounded by loving, positive people; I have never been happier.

People who live in the future often suffer from anxiety. In the past, I have almost been made homeless not once but twice over a short span, which were both terrifying experiences. My fear was that somewhen in the future, it is going to happen again.

I live in a small, rented flat, I have a lovely landlord, and the rent is cheap. My fear: what if my landlord wanted to sell up? I do not have much money to raise the capital for another flat (deposit, rent, and fees), it is an impossible task. If I did find another flat, who would take me? If they do a credit check, they will find out I am bankrupt. I do not have a guarantor, my council will not help me, the homeless are on the rise. I got myself into a right state, worrying about something that has not happened. I did this for years; I was so cruel to myself. Ask yourself, why put yourself through this? I now believe and trust my Spiritual Family to help me whenever I need it, they have never let me down.

When you start to love yourself, you begin to learn how to be kind to yourself, and therefore you let go of the fear.

You cannot change the PAST
but you can ruin the PRESENT
by worrying about the FUTURE
Luluvise

During a meditation Running Bear told me the "NOW" "PRESENT" is the most important time. If you feel as though you live in the past or the future, suffering from stress, anxiety, depression, bring your attention to NOW.

He advised going for some Healing, Reiki, Reflexology, Indian Head Massage. Try guided meditations, which are free on YouTube. I prefer the Jason Stephenson guided ones; his voice sends me off to the clouds. Instead of being in all the time, go out. I am lucky as I live close to a stony beach. Parking up and just watching the waves, whether stormy or sunny, helps me become present. Maybe you might live close to some woods, a park. Watch the trees sway to the rhythm of the wind.

True Story: Seagull
Most of us spend time in our car, queuing or crawling to our destination. Our minds can be consumed by the past or the future, filling us with dread. He told me in moments like this (not driving fast), take note of what is around you.

Look out of your window. Once when I was in a traffic jam, I saw on the grassy verge that separated the road right beside me, was seagull stamping his feet onto the ground, trying to imitate rain, so a worm could pop his head up.

I was fascinated with this intelligent little creature.

True Story: Beautiful Birds
One day I went to a car boot sale, my head was all over the place, full of dread and self-loathing. It was a beautiful sunny day, I did

not want to go, but my daughter and grandson were there selling their stuff.

I felt forced to go, but I knew I had to go along to support them. Feeling blue and consumed with my thoughts, I heard Running Bear telling me to look up. There was a big, beautiful hawk high above me being chased by two crows that seemed tiny compared to the hawk. I was fascinated, these two little crows chasing this massive hawk.

I stood there for at least ten minutes, just watching.

Nature brings us back to the Now, animals have a unique way of making us feel present. It is okay to have dreams, goals, and passion. Just try and be present, be grateful. During this you may have many beautiful epiphanies. Enjoy Now and all its wonders.

Realise deeply that the present moment is all you have.
Make the NOW the primary focus of your life.
Fearless Soul

Here are some of my favourite crystals that will help you stay in the Now. See if you can find one for yourself and sit and meditate with it, for a full explanation, please look at chapter "Crystal Healing":

➢ Amethyst – Tranquillity – Spiritual wisdom – Protection

➢ Fluorite – Helps the mind – Grounding – In the now

➢ Moonstone – New beginnings – Feminine power – Finding yourself – Success

➢ Rose Quartz – Love – Love yourself – Fertility – Healing

➢ Tiger Eye – Good luck – Success – Protection – Working with the universe

➢ Unakite – Healing – Grounding – Now – Dreams

Anger

Keeping hold of anger is destructive for our well-being and soul. I remember at a young age being so angry towards God. I was a good little girl and was taught bad things will only happen to you if you are naughty. From the ages of seven to ten years, I prayed to God every day, cried to him most nights, telling him that I was so good, why were these awful bad things keep happening to me?

In my early twenties, I had built up so much resentment and anger towards God. How could he let an innocent child suffer so much? I looked around at my environment, the world, so many people suffering. Why didn't God help? How could he allow this to happen?

One of the reasons I hated myself was because of him. My parents neglected me, how could an almighty powerful being abandon me?

Maybe I was not worthy? Perhaps I was not good enough? It might have been because I was ugly? Or was there something wrong with me?

It was not until later in life I learned it was me who had written my soul contract. It was me who had written all these terrible, cruel experiences for myself.

This time around, I had written several lifetimes into one. When this epiphany hit me all those years being angry at God, it was me who had written my story. I just laughed and laughed and joked when I return home to the spirit world, I will have a solemn word with myself. I now fully understand why the first forty odd years of my life were so painful that I had to learn and grow into the beautiful being I am today.

Joking aside, this anger I carried for many years just fuelled the self-loathing I had for myself. Keeping hold of it resulted in me suffering from health problems, mentally and physically.

Anger and resentment can damage your entire being, it takes a lot of your energy, letting go of it, and replacing it with Love; you will start to heal.

Exercise 7 "Anger"

When a negative situation arises, and you feel angry towards it, ask yourself, who does it hurt?

Write in your journal of your feelings, this is important as you will discover, holding onto this anger, you are only hurting yourself.

Ask yourself another question, do you deserve to feel this way?

Write some kind words, treat yourself like a dear friend, send love to yourself, and send positive healing thoughts to the person who has upset you. It may be hard at first, but by sending them love and healing out, you are letting go of your anger.

I had terrible road rage, I would shout and curse at people who would cut me up. There were times when I would get out of my car in anger, go and thump on their windows and give them a piece of my mind. If you are anything like me back then, you can probably relate to this.

Running Bear gave me some good advice: this temporary anger is destructive to our soul, not only does it affect you, but it also affects other people. He told me next time someone angers you, especially on the road, immediately say out loud, "I'm sending you love and healing." By saying this, you are letting go of the anger, replacing love, which changes your demeanour.

I have been practicing this for several years, it can be challenging at times but sending out the good vibes works. Give it a go?

Anger is an acid that can do more harm to the vessel
in which it is stored that to anything on which it is poured.
Mark Twain

Here are some of my favourite crystals that will help you with releasing your anger. See if you can find one for yourself and sit and meditate with it, for a full explanation, please look at chapter "Crystal Healing":

➢ Amethyst – Tranquillity – Spiritual wisdom – Protection
➢ Banded Agate – Good Luck – Wealth – Healing
➢ Blue Kyanite – Trusting yourself – Psychic ability – Dreaming
➢ Caribbean Calcite – Communication with spirit
➢ Larimar – Communication – Finding your path – Healing

Forgiveness

Yes, forgiveness is a hard word to say, hear, or read. My tummy used to curdle and tense at the very thought of this word. How could I ever forgive those that harmed me in such a cruel and vile manner? You are probably thinking the same. The truth is, it is not about forgiving them, it is about forgiving YOURSELF. When we experience pain, we store this into our souls, which in time can manifest in all sorts of horrible emotions such as anger, shame, guilt, resentment, etc. In some strange way holding onto this festering pain can play havoc with your mental and physical health. You have thoughts that maybe you deserved it. Perhaps if you had done things differently, it would not have happened. You feel all or partially responsible. The cruel words from your abusers are still fresh in your mind "you are an idiot," "you are fat," "you are ugly." These small words twist and turn in our thoughts, making us think that we are inadequate that we are horrible beings. So, I am not asking you to forgive those that have hurt you, I want you to start today. FORGIVE YOURSELF.

True Story: The Abortion
I was fifteen and pregnant. My parents were furious with me; they wanted to keep it a secret as they did not want to bring shame to the family. So, I was walking on eggshells; my father never spoke to me; he just kept giving me deathly stares. My mother was busily fussing around me.

"I need to take you to the doctors and get rid of that thing."

She glanced down at my stomach.

I was in a whirlwind of torment; I really wanted my baby, the very thought of getting rid of it scorched my soul.

"Mum, I want to keep my baby; both Reece and I have decided to have it," I whispered to my mother, hoping Dad would not hear.

Mum exploded, hissing and spitting her vile words out of her mouth. "If you have this baby, we will throw you out. You will have to live in the gutters with the rats. How will you feed your baby? You stupid little girl." I burst into tears and ran to my bedroom.

Later that evening, Reece showed up, and I told him what my mother had said. I could not believe what came out of his mouth. He originally wanted this baby as much as I did until now.

"I think I am too young to be a father; how will we look after it?"

I was devasted and crushed. I cradled my belly and wished that I could have a happy ending. But, unfortunately for me, Reece ended our relationship and left me in tears.

The next morning mum had me up at the doctor's; she sat beside me and told him that I was pregnant. The old doctor with whirly eyebrows and thick rim glasses looked down his nose at me.

"Tutt Tutt, you have got yourself into trouble. Obviously, I will book you in for an abortion."

"Yes!" Mum snapped.

"But I don't want to have one," I whispered shamelessly.

Mum exploded with the doctor agreeing to everything. She scolded me. I felt so alone, so afraid, so I went along with it.

I was put into a gown and was told by the nurse not to mention to the other patients what I was in for as they could turn nasty towards me. As you can imagine being so young, I was terrified; all I wanted was my baby.

I was taken on a bed down to the surgical room. The nurse told me the anaesthetist will be out shortly. As soon as she left and was out of sight, this was my chance to escape. I sat up and swung my legs to the side; as soon as I did, a lady appeared from the surgical room.

"What are you doing?"

"I'm not going through with this." I jumped down from the bed.

The lady shouted something, and before I knew it, four people were wrestling me to the bed and pinning me down. I screamed and screamed that I wanted my baby. I fought them with all my might, but it was useless. The anaesthetist stuck the cannula into my hand and injected the aesthetic; I was knocked out.

Opening my eyes, Mum was sat beside my bed. She looked worried. I felt a heavy period pain in my tummy; my baby was gone.

"Are you okay, Max?"

"No! No!" I cried hugging my tum.

I went home and was told to never mention this incident to anyone; we must brush it under the carpet and get on with our lives.

I hated my parents for what they did to me; I was so angry that they had taken my baby. It was not long, just after my sixteenth birthday, I left home. I was filled with so many different emotions, anger, shame, guilt was a huge one for me. For the next two years, I hardly had contact with my parents until I was eighteen and pregnant. I was overjoyed; I had my own place, no one nor anyone was going to take my baby away. I told this to my parents, and if they want to be a part of my child's life, they could. It was hard to forgive them at first, but my mum and dad were smitten with their little granddaughter.

Sadly, Dad passed after Elisha's third birthday, but I went on to have another four children with Reece. Mum found a lovely man who is a great grandfather to my children.

28 April 2020 was my mum's birthday. She lived in a warden control complex; Covid had us locked down. My children and their children made a beautiful banner, we all went up to the complex, mum could see us safely through the glass window as we held up the banner and sang happy birthday to her.

It was a magical moment; looking around, I could feel the love they had for my mother. I could have disowned my parents for what they did to me, never seeing them again or letting them see their grandchildren, but instead of hating them, which did not serve me, I choose to forgive.

I heard Running Bear in my ear; this is what forgiveness does; it opens your heart to love.

True Story: The Judge
When I had to attend court to repossess my family home, I had to sit opposite a strict, cold, unfriendly smart woman, who looked down her nose at me.

You can imagine how I felt, I was a bag of nerves, full of self-loathing, a failure but most of all, shameful. This condescending Judge looked at the details in front of her and said, "You silly little girl, you have gotten yourself into a pickle." She ordered me out of my home within two weeks. I tried to barter for four weeks as I had no home to go to and dependent children. "No! Two weeks" I felt anger, I felt panic, I felt all sort of horrible things. For years afterward, I hated the Judge, not for the repossession but the way she made me felt, I thought the Judge was cruel and belittling, but the underlying problem was not the Judge, it was me, I could not handle feeling a failure. I suffered terribly with this pain festering inside me, too scared and shameful to tell others how I felt. It was easy to blame the Judge, but it was hard to look at and accept my own emotions.

This self-love journey is the best path you will ever take, but it can also be the hardest.

Once you accept what has happened, except that it is okay to make mistakes. We are beings with many emotions, evaluate them and learn, only then can we release the pain from our soul and begin to grow.

Exercise 8 "Forgiveness"
Running Bear told me to write myself a little note, it can be in your journal, mobile, iPad, etc. Go back to a pain that you hold onto, in this instant, the repossession order. First, accept the past, you cannot change it. Write down how you felt, and in the second column, treat yourself like a dear friend, as mentioned in the previous chapter.

Shameful	You were so brave.
Judged	You are a wonderful, beautiful being.
Belittled	You would never treat anyone like this.
Failure	You have come so far, I am so proud.
Wanted to die	I am elated that you are alive.

I FORGIVE MYSELF – I FORGIVE MYSELF – I FORGIVE MYSELF

If you need help with this, ask a dear friend to help you. Read this little note to yourself for twenty-one days straight, these lovely comments in the second column will start to wash the pain from your soul. Some of you may need longer, so I recommend thirty days. Write in your journal how you felt before this exercise and after, you will see a huge difference. You can repeat this exercise as many times as you want, each time, there will be a difference. Remember, it is not a race or a competition, I had to repeat this task a few times over two years. The human soul is like an onion with layers and layers, it is not an overnight fix, take your time, and you will get there.

Once you start to forgive yourself, you will start to view the people who harmed you in the past differently. You will realise that you do not deserve to carry this destructive pain. It will become evident, the ones that hurt us are in pain too. I have had people do terrible things to me in the past, such as being raped, beaten, betrayed, etc., but once I started to forgive myself, I found myself sending out thoughts of healing and love to all of them. It is okay not to forget, though, as these are your lessons. We all know not to put your hands into the fire, you will get burned, so we will not be doing that again.

A note from Running Bear
When people hurt you, whether intentionally or unintentionally, you have the beautiful ability to heal and forgive. You will also learn a valuable lesson not to hate but to prevent their behaviour from destroying your soul. Forgiveness is the highest form of love, and in return, you will receive the abundance of untold

peace and happiness.

Here are some of my favourite crystals that will help you with forgiveness. See if you can find one for yourself and sit and meditate with it. For a full explanation, please look at chapter "Crystal Healing":

> ➢ Blue Lace Agate – Communication
> ➢ Merlinite – Magic – Self-discovery – Spiritual Growth – Forgiveness
> ➢ Morganite – New love – Healing heart
> ➢ Orac Agate – Go with the Flow – Healing – Forgiveness
> ➢ Rose Quartz – Love – Love yourself – Fertility – Healing
> ➢ Sunset Aura Quartz – Joy – Let Go – Positivity

Gut Intuition

Your Gut Intuition is your inner soul trying to steer you on the right path. Everyone has had this feeling at some point in their lives. It is your soul speaking to you, trying to help you on your life's journey, but two main obstacles are in your way. Your head and heart play a vital role in hindering our decisions.

Your head is full of wavering thoughts, trying to rationalise the situations, whereas your heart is full of emotions, whether it is negative or positive. Usually, in Givers, the heart rules the head, with this combination causing self-doubt, so it is natural to ignore our first instinct, our Gut Intuition.

What does your gut feeling feel like?

A gut feeling can be a different sensation for each person. Some may experience a definite sinking feeling in the middle of the solar plexus, feeling that something is not quite right, or you can feel a strong surge from your stomach, feeling alarmed, or a strong urge to fix or change something. Others can experience a gnawing in the gut, telling us to go home in a different way.

Everyone has a gut feeling about something. Have you had a strong feeling while driving that you should turn left at the junction instead of your usual, right? Only to ignore it. "I'm not turning left, that is a long way home," only to find out by going your usual way there is a significant traffic jam. Now you are kicking yourself as you sit in the heavy traffic, if you had turned left, you would have been home by now. Your Guides, Angels, and your beautiful Spiritual Family often communicate via your

Gut Intuition. They are whispering, giving us signs to help us, but you ignore it on most occasions, not because you are ignorant. It is because you do not believe in yourself. You may have had someone in your life now or in the past that has hurt your heart and told you lies to confuse you. Due to this, you are always second-guessing yourself.

True Story: Chole
My good friend wanted me to meet her new boyfriend. When I finally met him, my tummy twisted and turned, my gut told me he was a bad man.

With that, I took my Chole to one side and told her not to trust him, he was just out for himself. She told me I was being silly and tried to convince me he was a lovely man. My head became confused. Did I get it wrong? Was I being mean? Was I silly? I apologise to my friend, I felt foolish. Six months later, my friend found out that he was a con artist and had cleared her bank account of thousands of pounds and almost crippled her business. How did you know? She asked me, I was as shocked as her.

There are countless times when my gut has told me something only for my head to dismiss it, or other people telling me I had got it wrong. I believed them, as I lacked confidence within myself.

We do not listen to ourselves because we are good people, we would never treat others in an ill manner, so when our gut talks to us, giving us a warning, we dismiss it as we only want to see the good in people.

When I first met my husband, my gut immediately told me, "No, stay away, he is bad for you." I was only fourteen at the time, so I dismissed it.

In my late thirties, when I met my second husband

immediately, my gut told me the same thing. I told myself, do not be silly, he is a lovely man, a police officer, good morals, etc. Boy, did I get this wrong. I should have listened to myself.

Self-doubt is your brain telling you otherwise, playing on your weakness, your self-loathing, making you confused, and questioning your judgment. I bet every time you had that strong feeling in your gut, it turned out right?

I had two very harsh lessons with both marriages.

Both abusive and were cheating on me; while my gut told me so, my head told me otherwise, my heart filled up with pain, I was in a whirlwind of torment.

True Story: Alan

After my last divorce, I made an oath to myself, I am now going to listen to my gut. I am no longer going to question or ignore it, as I have realised avoiding it can incur many painful experiences. One evening my mother invited me to her local pub where she played darts, it was an unusual request as this was not our norm, but I went anyway. I had a feeling she was up to something.

Sitting beside her in her surroundings with her friends, my mother loudly told me that I was useless at getting a man and had poor judgment in men. What was she playing at? She was embarrassing me in front of her friends, laughing at me, with hypercritical eyes. She then bellowed out to Alan, who was in his forties, a similar age to me.

He came to the table. "He wants to take you out for a drink." my mother looked smug.

I was somewhat shocked and outraged. "You can't get yourself a decent man. Alan is a good man." What? I do not want a man; I am happy on my own. How dare she?

Instantly, looking at this man, my tummy twisted and turned, my gut told me to stay away, he was not good. I just got up and left. The next morning my mother was on the phone, telling me off for my rude behaviour, and that I should give Alan a chance. I stuck to my guns, no way would I ever entertain him.

My advice to you if your gut is telling you something, go with it. BELIEVE.

Three months later, I switched on the TV, the news was on, which I do not usually watch, but Running Bear told me not to turn over the channel. I could not believe my eyes; Alan's face was on TV. I turned up the volume, he had been arrested for severely attacking his girlfriend, slashed her face, and ripped out her eye. I stood there in shock.

I telephoned Mum and told her about the news. Mum replied, "Well, his girlfriend does have a vial mouth on her." I could not believe what she had said. It does not matter what she had said, no one deserves to be attacked like that.

All I can say, thank god I believe in myself, just imagine if I self-doubted myself. That poor woman could have been me. So please, believe in yourself, stick to your guns, dismiss those self-doubting thoughts, as each time you believe in yourself, you will get stronger and more confident. It does not matter if someone is standing in your face telling you are wrong. You are not, so what if they call you stubborn. That is what my mother called me when I refused to go out with Alan, so stand by your true self.

True Story: Real Monsters
I was fifteen years old, and I had only been dating Reece for a couple of months. He asked me to a family function, and I was nervous at the idea of meeting his parents, let alone the rest of his family.

"What if they don't like me?" I worried.

"They will, you're lovely!" Reece reassured me.

The night of the function, my tummy was in knots. I did not want to go, I wished I could stay at home. I felt nervous, and I knew something terrible would happen. The venue was close by, and we made our own way there. I was greeted by his parents, and the knots in my stomach started to calm down. They seemed nice, down to earth sort of people-friendly, and chatty. I felt slightly more at ease as Reece began to introduce me to the rest of his family.

I notice a tall, dark-haired man, skinny in appearance, making his way over to me while I stood and chatted to Reece's mum and aunty.

"This is our brother Roy," Reece's mum said, introducing me to the tall, lanky, dark-haired man.

He grabbed my hand to kiss it. Suddenly I was overwhelmed by one of the most horrible feelings I have ever experienced. I felt I was drowning in a sewer. It made me want to heave, it made me gag, I could not breathe. I felt violated as awful images flashed through my mind. It was disgusting what he was doing to his young daughters. Not able to contain myself, I snatched my hand back before he could place his slimy lips on me.

"YOU'RE A NONCE!" I screamed.

I heard everyone gasp around me. I did not care, I just wanted to get away from him. Bolting from the building at lightning speed, I felt relief as the cold wind swept on to my face. I stood outside, taking in the cold air, and felt I could finally breathe. I could feel my body trembling, I felt so dirty my whole body seemed to be covered in filth. All I wanted was a scalding hot shower and to scrub myself with a razor. Those horrible images kept popping into my mind, and squeezing my eyes shut, I tried to block them out.

"I can't believe you just did that!" Reece stood behind me, he sounded furious.

I turned to face him, and he was shocked at the state I was in. He had never seen me like that before.

"Maxine, what's wrong?" his voice softened.

I felt a tear roll down my cheek.

"I'm sorry... I'm sorry!" I started to sob.

"It's okay... but you can't go round calling people a nonce... you can get in trouble for that." Reece's voice was stern.

Holding my breath and trying to calm myself down, I looked deeply into his eyes.

"I'm sorry... I can't go back in there!"

"Yes, you can... don't be silly... all you need to do is apologise!"

"Apologise?" I laughed.

"You've got to be joking, there is no way that I am ever going anywhere near your uncle!"

"Maxine!" Reece scolded.

"I'm going home. I'll see you later!"

"You can't!"

I was true to my word. Even though Reece and I got married, I never went near his uncle. When I had recently given birth to our third daughter Brooke, seven years later, we had decided to go for a meal with his parents one Sunday afternoon. We arranged to meet at his parents' house and arrived slightly early. I was sitting on the living room floor playing with my daughters while waiting for his mum to finish her morning shift. She usually came home by midday but glancing down at my watch, I noticed it was half-past one. I heard Reece's dad murmur to him.

"Where the bloody hell is your mother? I'm starving!"

As soon as he said it, I heard the front door slam. When she walked into the room, Reece's mum looked devastated. Reece jumped to his feet and rushed over to her.

"Mum, are you OK?"

"No! No!" We could hardly hear her.

"Mum, sit down." Reece guided her to the settee, where she slumped herself down.

There was an awkward silence, and all eyes transfixed on her.

"It's your uncle... uncle Roy, he's been arrested... for sexually abusing his girls... apparently, it's been going on for years." She was stunned and shocked.

"YOU KNEW! How did you know?" Reece's father shouted at me.

I was startled and taken aback by his abrupt, loud behaviour.

All eyes were now on me. Feeling uneasy, I concentrated on the floor.

"How did you know?" he demanded.

"I don't know, I just did," I whispered, hoping the floor would open and swallow me.

Start today, trust your gut intuition, listen to what your soul is telling you. You are powerful, just tune into the vibrations all around you, listen to the whispers of your Spiritual Family trying to guide you.

True Story: It is Not Flu

In 1989, just after a cold, bitter Christmas, I was twenty years old with a two-year-old little girl called Elisha. The weather was cold and harsh – a breeding ground for bacteria. After a couple of weeks, everyone I knew was starting to feel better, except Dad. He seemed to be getting worse. One morning I popped round to see my parents, and Mum opened the front door. As I struggled to get the buggy through the doorway, I was shocked and mortified as my eyes were drawn to Dad. I could see him sitting in his armchair, bending over, trying to put his slippers on. Watching him puffing and panting, I was suddenly hit by a bolt of lightning. This feeling, this sensation that struck my body, burned fiercely in my stomach.

The overwhelming thought bellowed the words out of my mouth.

"There's something seriously wrong with Dad!"

Leaving Elisha and Mum in the hallway, I dashed into the living room.

"Let me put these on for you!"

I crouched down in front of him and slipped his feet, encased in his Christmas socks, into his new navy velour slippers. I could see the relief as Dad flopped himself back into his armchair, heavily wheezing. The feeling in my stomach was still surging strongly, and I knew I had to get him help.

"You need to ring the doctor! He's not right," I told Mum, who was utterly startled by my assertive behaviour.

"There's nothing wrong with me… don't fuss," Dad gasped.

Hearing his words, the feeling in my stomach surged even stronger. There was something seriously wrong with him. Not backing down, I wanted him to seek medical help, and I gave mum a fierce gaze.

"Mum! Get on that phone and get an appointment immediately!" I demanded.

"Don't you dare, Pearl," Dad challenged her.

Mum could see I would not take no for an answer, but she could also see her husband's fury. Dad never went to the doctor, he had probably only seen a doctor three times in his life, and he was not going to break a habit of a lifetime.

Finally, Mum made a snap decision and telephoned the doctor's surgery. Dad was furious but too weak to argue. Getting an appointment at the drop of a hat was an easy task for Mum. Her best friend was the head receptionist; there was no 'ring back after two p.m. ;' there was no 'we do not have an appointment available for another two weeks;' it was a case of 'when?'

"Got to be there in ten minutes, seeing Dr Kelly," Mum confirmed.

"Who?" I asked curiously. I had never heard of him.

In the background, I could hear Dad growling under his breath; he certainly was not happy that Mum had agreed with me.

"Pam says he's one of the new doctors, apparently he's really nice." We both ignored Dad.

Bending over Dad's feet, I took his slippers off and put his shoes on. I could feel him resisting me, but I gave him a glare, and he surrendered unhappily, continuing to moan and groan under his breath. After putting on his shoes, I jumped to my feet and got his thick winter coat.

"You're not coming with me!" he gasped for air.

"Oh yes, I am!" I was adamant.

"No, you're not!" he coughed. He was getting angry.

"Yes, I am!" I argued back.

"Right, I won't go!" He slumped back down into his armchair, breathing heavily.

It became a staring competition – neither of us was blinking. Suddenly Mum intervened; she knew that we were both as stubborn as one another.

"Look, Maxine, why don't you stay here while I take your dad to the Docs?" Mum compromised.

Breaking the trance, I saw reason.

"OK, I will wait here!" I watched Dad struggle out of his armchair, and it made my heart flinch. I did not like seeing my dad so weak... so ill. I helped him with his coat while he continued breathlessly to protest.

Waving them goodbye, I returned to the living room, switched on the TV, and selected a channel that was playing cartoons. Elisha sat on the settee, transfixed by the TV screen. I was too worried to able to sit, biting the inside of my lip frantically.

I kept checking my wristwatch... fifteen minutes, twenty minutes had passed. Suddenly the front door opened, and in walked Dad looking pale and exhausted and still gasping for air. He made a beeline for his armchair, collapsing in it, still wearing his coat; he did not have the energy to remove it.

"Well?" I looked at Mum.

"It's flu!" Mum replied.

With that, I spun and looked at Dad. So much fury built up into my stomach, I thought I was going to explode like an erupting volcano.

"He doesn't have the flu!" I shouted.

"There is something seriously wrong with him," I continued to scream.

"It's just the flu," Dad gasped at me.

"Get another appointment... I want him to see a different doctor." The burning feeling in my stomach roared, I knew that I was right.

"What?" both parents were astounded.

I stood my ground until Mum picked up the phone and got another appointment. Dad was furious with me. He had never wanted to go to the Doctors in the first place; there was no way he was going again. But the burning feeling in my stomach remained fierce, and I watched both parents leave the house again.

Elisha was so good. Not once had she bothered me, she remained still and quiet, glued to the TV; she was oblivious to what was going on around her. Again, I started to wait patiently, pacing the floor while biting my lip harder and making it bleed. This gut feeling was so strong, I was so anxious. Suddenly the front door opened, I went rushing to the door. Mum greeted me, but she looked shocked and distressed.

"Where's Dad?" I asked, glancing over her shoulder.

"Look, don't go out there… he's in the car… he doesn't want to see you." Mum tried to remain calm.

"What? Why? What's wrong?" I panicked.

"Maxine! Please stay in here. I have just got to get his pyjamas and slippers. He's got to go to hospital… IMMEDIATELY!"

I was stunned and speechless as I watched Mum quickly collect his belongings.

"Look, I will give you a call later and let you know what's going on," she promised.

I wanted to know now, but I also knew deep down that I had to let her get on with it. It was not the time to be selfish. Watching her go off with Dad was so hard; my body filled with worry. I could not help thinking the worse now all my fears had been confirmed, but what was eating me up was the need to know what was wrong with him. How bad was he? Can they save him? Was he going to die? I wish I could be there for him, but I knew him too well.

"Hospitals are not a place for children," he would have said.

I waited patiently for the call, but Mum never rang.

Why didn't she ring? Was he terribly ill? Too bad to leave

his side. Was he dying?

That time waiting at Mum's seemed to be one of the longest days of my life. Eventually, at nine p.m., Mum fell through the front door, she looked exhausted. Elisha had curled up on the couch and fallen fast asleep. used one of the blankets that I had stored under the pushchair and had neatly tucked her in.

Mum sat gently next to Elisha, giving her a loving look.

"She is beautiful, a sleeping Angel." Mum smiled at her.

I looked at Mum; I was so desperate to find out about Dad, but instead of interrogating her, I offered her a much-needed cup of tea. We sat down with a cuppa each, and Mum whispered what had happened.

The second appointment was with Dr Adams, the main man. It was his practice, which he had established twenty years ago. He was a mature man who was stern but gentle.

When I was a young girl, I kept getting tonsillitis. One time I saw Dr Adams, and he was brilliant with me; he was alarmed at how many times I had contracted the illness, and it was he who organised the operation for having my tonsils taken out. He was a man of action; he did not like his patients suffering.

Dr Adams glanced through my Dad's thin medical notes; he was surprised to see him.

"You have just been up here? Dr Kelly has put down that you have the flu, hmmm… is this correct?" he looked puzzled.

"Yes, that's right… I… er… wanted a second opinion," Mum spoke for Dad, feeling somewhat embarrassed.

"OK… I don't have to ask what the problem is with your husband… you can see he's finding it hard to breathe… let us listen to your chest." Dr Adams picked up his stethoscope and asked Mum if she could help him remove Dad's coat. Lifting Dad's jumper, he placed his cold instrument against his chest.

"It's flu," Dad gasped.

"Just take deep breaths." Dr Adams listened to his chest.

Dad kept coughing; he could not take a deep breath. He was constantly wheezing. Dr Adams' face dropped; the seriousness in his voice spoke volumes.

Placing the stethoscope around his neck, he looked furious.

"Did Dr Kelly listen to your chest Mr Booker?" he asked in a stern, firm voice.

"Yeah," Dad coughed.

Dr Adams quickly picked up his phone.

"I want an ambulance for Mr Booker immediately!" he ordered the receptionist.

"What?" Mum exclaimed.

"Your husband doesn't have flu… he has fluid on his lungs." He was a man on a vital mission.

"He has to go into hospital now, this is serious!"

"He has to go into hospital. Right now?" Mum was shocked.

"Dr Kelly did listen to your chest?" His face flushed red with anger.

"Yeah," Mum replied. Dad was too stunned to talk.

"Right… excuse me, Mr… Mrs Booker!" The furious doctor stormed out of his office.

Mum could not believe her eyes as Dr Adams stormed into the office opposite his. Dr Kelly was on a break, sitting at his desk drinking a cup of coffee; he looked shocked and startled as the raging doctor came charging in at him.

"You f*****g stupid incompetent b*****! Mr Booker is seriously ill! He does not have the f*****g flu! You are an idiot! He has got fluid on his lungs! You are sacked! Get your stuff and get out of my practice before you kill someone!"

Dr Adams stormed back into his office in emergency mode.

"I do apologise for my behaviour Mr and Mrs Booker... I am sorry, but I cannot have doctors like that in my practice... listening to your chest, you can hear easily that your lungs are filled with fluid... he should have picked it up... I'm telling you it's a good job you came back."

A receptionist popped her head around the door, saying the ambulance was only five minutes away. The realisation hit Dad; he started to panic. His pride kicked in and his fear of hospitals.

"Listen, Pearl, I don't want to go into hospital," he whispered, praying the doctor would not hear him.

"Mr Booker, you're extremely ill! You will have to have your chest drained, plus there will be further investigations. There is a reason why your chest is filling up with fluid, we have to find out why... anyway, the hospital is the best place for you." Dr Adams tried to reassure Dad.

Suddenly Dad panicked.

"I don't want to wear one of those gowns with my arse hanging out!" He looked terrified.

Both Mum and Dr Adams tried to persuade him that was the least of his worries, but Dad was adamant. He was a proud man, and, as for the ambulance, he refused to go into it.

He was convinced that he was not that bad, and the ambulance could be used for someone else who needed it more than he did. Dr Adams could see how stressed and upset my Dad was getting, so they negotiated. The ambulance was cancelled; the doctor agreed that he could go home and get his pyjamas and slippers on one condition – that he would have to go straight to the hospital afterward. Dad agreed, and Dr Adams phoned the hospital to make the arrangements. In the car home, he told Mum that he did not want me there.

After Mum quickly popped home, she drove to the hospital

where a porter with a wheelchair and a doctor patiently waited for Dad.

He was immediately given a chest drain.

The consultant told Mum that she was lucky to get him in when she did. He told her another twenty-four hours, and Dad would have drowned in his own fluids.

A few days later, the doctors at the hospital found that Dad had cancer in the lungs, he lived for another one and a half years.

A note from your Angel

I am here, whispering into your soul, trust your gut intuition.

When something looks amazing, I will let you know if it is no good.

If there is something wrong, I will tell you.

Please listen.

Here are some of my favourite crystals that will help you with your intuition. See if you can find one for yourself and sit and meditate with it. For a full explanation, please look at chapter "Crystal Healing":

➢ Blue Kyanite – Trusting yourself – Psychic ability – Dreaming

➢ Chevron Amethyst – Spiritual – Peace – Protection – Best version of yourself

➢ Labradorite – Spiritual Growth – Magic – Trust in spirit

➢ Merlinite – Magic – Self-discovery – Spiritual Growth – Forgiveness

➢ Moonstone – New beginnings – Feminine power – Finding yourself – Success

Angels

Everyone is born with their own loving Angel, who will walk beside you until you return to your Spiritual Home. Some of you may be sensitive to spirit, it does not matter if you are not, after reading this, your Angel is going to be thrilled, as you will now know their signs, such as falling white feathers or finding them in unusual places. Seeing Angel's numbers such as 1111 everywhere. They communicate through dreams, so take note, and write it down your dreams in your journal, it might not make sense right now, but it may be a message for your future self. Look out for signs in the clouds and coins on the ground. Some of you may have been fortunate like me to have seen them in their purest form.

True Story: My Angel

One early morning, it must have been about two a.m., I was awoken by a bright light at the end of my bed. Opening my sleepy eyes, it only took a few moments to focus on a magnificent, big, dazzling cloud that had beautiful vibrant colours shooting through it like sparks of electricity. Observing this glowing mass of energy, I instantly thought the moon had reflected onto my mirrors, causing this phenomenon. Then I noticed my curtains were shut, so I assumed it was a ghost.

I was not frightened or scared, it had a loving, soothing, and warm vibration. Saying goodnight to it, I cuddled my duvet and went back to sleep.

The next day I carried on with my regular daily routine, not mentioning a word to anyone about what I had seen earlier. Surprisingly, I received a telephone call from a friend I met eighteen months ago at a psychic fair, she was a brilliant medium. We instantly hit it off and swapped telephone numbers, but we both lost touch due to our busy schedules.

She asked me if I had any plans for the evening as she wanted to pop round and see me. I was delighted. I remembered she loved pizza, so I invited her round for tea. I was so excited to see her, she was a lovely young woman in her late twenties.

The last time I saw her, her little boy was only six months old.

That evening I ordered a couple of large pizzas. It was great to see Lucy. Mostly the topic of conversation was about her pride and joy, who was now walking and talking.

I never once mentioned the ghost I had seen earlier.

"Maxine… I have a message for you!"

"Do you?" I was startled.

"This morning, I was told I should contact you immediately."

"Really?" I was a bit worried. What was wrong?

"You didn't see a ghost this morning?"

My jaw dropped.

"It was an Angel!"

I was dumbfounded and lost for words as she continued to tell me in detail what I had seen that morning. Everything was accurate.

"I… saw… an… Angel?" I was still in shock.

"Yes! It wasn't a ghost!" she giggled.

"But… don't Angels have wings and a halo?" I was confused.

"No! Angels can come in many different forms... you happen to see it in its natural form!"

"Have you seen an Angel?"

"No, I haven't been that lucky!"

"But why me? What did it want from me?" I asked, still feeling confused.

"You have Angels walking with you! You are going to help a lot of people!"

"Me? Are you sure of that?"

"Yeah, I'm sure!" She smiled.

A lot of people do not know that when we feel despair, sadness, fear, and vulnerability, we can ask our Angels for help in these times.

True Story: Help!

A while ago, in my fledgling days one Sunday evening, I had to be at Jane's house for six p.m., she would take me to one of her venues where she was going to conduct a spiritual service. She wanted to take me so I could do the platform work. I was anxious at the thought of being on stage and giving out messages for spirits. I did not mind doing it in our circle group, I felt comfortable as I knew them all, but to get up in front of strangers... I was terrified! What if I do not get any messages? I did not want to stand there looking like a complete plonker. Jane reassured me and told me I would be brilliant, I wished I had her confidence.

I had left in plenty of time to get to Jane's house. I was unsure where she lived, but from the verbal instructions she gave me, it seemed relatively straightforward (this was before sat nav days). It was a dark, cold night, and although I was following her directions, I had a horrible feeling I was heading in the wrong direction – travelling further and further down the road, I was going out of the city into rural land.

Everything seemed so dark and eerie, and it did not help to have the car behind me driving right up my rear.

Seeing a right-hand turn, I indicated and drove into Sandy Lane while the impatient driver accelerated off. I pulled over and glanced at the time, it was ten to six, my heart started to race as panic set in. I put on my interior light, and everything around me looked pitch black. A shiver ran up my spine, I was lost, and I felt extremely vulnerable. I quickly pulled my a-z map book out of the glove department and looked up the lane. I was devastated to find it was not on the map!

I was getting anxious. I could not telephone Jane, she had been cut off.

What was I going to do? Feeling lost and frantic, I prayed. Please send me someone to help me.

Suddenly a small police car appeared beside me. Unwinding my window, the friendly police officer asked me if I was OK.

"No! I'm lost!" I felt embarrassed and relieved simultaneously.

"Where are you going?"

I told him the address.

"You're way off. I tell you what, I'm headed in that direction, why don't you follow me?"

I could not believe my ears; I was so grateful.

Arriving at my destination, the friendly police officer beeped his horn and waved me goodbye.

Looking at the time, it was dead at six p.m. Yes, I had made it in time. Thank you!

Jane opened her door; I could not wait to tell her what had

just happened.

"What do you mean a police car showed up?" she scolded.

I was taken aback by her sharpness.

"I followed the police officer here," I said, feeling somewhat confused.

"Police? Are you sure?" she interrogated me.

"Yeah!" What was her problem?

"I have lived here for twenty-five years... I have never seen a police car... Roy! Have you?" Jane shouted to her husband, who was standing behind her, putting on his coat.

"Nope, we don't have police here!" They both stared at me as though I was mad.

At the service that night, Jane asked me if I had any messages for anyone.

A man was sitting in the crowd, he must have been in his forties. I had visions that he drove a small white van, the rear left tyre came out in 3D. I was shown he travelled up and down the motorway every day, but suddenly they showed me his rear tyre exploding. I told the man he had a small white van, and he nodded in agreement. I told him he used the motorway each day to travel to work, again, he nodded. Before he went to work tomorrow morning, I told him to get his rear left tyre checked.

He thanked me and told me he would do so.

A couple of weeks later, I received feedback from the service. The man I had told to check his tyre sent his gratitude, he took his van to the garage the next morning, where the technician found a severe fault with the rear left tyre.

A year later, I met up with an old friend for coffee, who was a Police Officer. I told her about my incident how this lovely Officer came to my rescue.

A few days later she called me.

"You know your police story? Was it about asking for help, or was it a ghost story?"

"What? It was about asking for help. Being lost out in the forest was scary, if a police officer had not shown up, there is no way I would have wound my window down for anyone else. The only bizarre thing… thinking about it… was that he instantly appeared beside me when I asked for help. Being in a dark lane, I thought his headlights would have startled me, or I would have heard his car. Anyway, why do you ask?"

"I received a police circular stating a police officer was killed on duty in that area several years ago, since then, there have been sightings of him and stories that he is still helping!"

True Story: Angel Healing

Angels are mighty, and asking them to help, extraordinary things can occur, like my lovely Police Officer helping me in times of need. Angels are the only ones that can interfere in our lives, they are messengers from God, they have the power to execute miracles, and with me, they have performed many.

When I was forty-eight years old, I was only given three months to live. I have Mixed Hyperlipidaemia, and my Triglycerides scored thirty. The consultant told me it would take five years to get my lipids down and said I was at a high risk of having a fatal heart attack. This was a scary time for me, during this period, I got my affairs in order, setting up and planning my funeral. I was working in the finance industry and had to be signed off from work. Even though this was a dark time for me, I had some remarkable experiences during this period.

One afternoon, I was sat on the sofa all by myself.

Suddenly, a massive Angel wing swooped from behind me across my living room. With its mighty power, it blew wind into my face making me blink. I was astounded. A few days later, again on the sofa, I moved, but there was an angelic face on my left shoulder. It made me jump at first, but again I could not believe it.

A good friend of mine, who is a lovely healer, came to mine to do some healing. I never told her about my experiences from the week before.

Placing her hands above my solar plexus, she was amazed. She told me she had never felt this energy before. "It's angelic, you have an Angel wrapped around you." She was excited. A couple of weeks later, after having more blood tests, I had to see the doctor. My doctor was thrilled to see me, she could not wait to tell me, "It's a miracle," she exclaimed. My Triglycerides had remarkably returned to normal; I was no longer on death's door.

My advice to you is to talk to your Angel, ask for their guidance, ask for their help, you can ask them for healing for yourself or others. Watch out for the miracles that unfold for you.

True Story: The Message

As the door slowly crept open, I picked up my hard, lumpy teddy bear, ready to launch it at my unsuspecting brother.

At weekends or during school holidays, my dad would enforce the law.

"If either of you are caught out of your bedrooms or wake your mother or me before eight a.m., you will get this!"

My Dad held his huge fist up, clenching a thick leather cowboy belt, and waved it violently in our faces.

At this time, my brother was only five, and I was six, we would never contemplate waking Dad up before eight or even venture downstairs!

My brother was a very timid boy who would jump at his own

102

shadow, he never liked to be on his own, which resulted in him coming into my bedroom and curling up with me.

The sun shone brightly through my bedroom window, casting a sunny shadow throughout my room. I could hear all the birds singing as they perched themselves on Mum's long washing line. I had been awake for at least an hour and estimated it must have been about seven thirty a.m. It was Saturday; I had to wait patiently for my parents to rise.

Time back then seemed to be so slow.

I was wide awake and so bored just sitting on my bed, waiting!

I was ready with the teddy bear; I was trying to contain my excitement and laughter. I knew hurling the teddy bear at my brother was going to frighten the life out of him. The door crept open. It was not my brother that entered my room, it was…

A panda bear walking on its hind legs.

I could not believe my eyes. I dropped the teddy and retreated to the corner of my headboard and curled up into a small ball of fright!

The panda moved slowly towards me and extended his front paw.

"Don't be scared, Maxine."

Not only did it walk, but it also spoke to me! Fear raced through my body at lightning speed; my heart pounded hard in my chest.

I felt as though it was going to burst out! I wanted to scream for Mum, but another fear ran through my small body, I must not wake Dad.

I trembled with fright as the panda approached, not knowing what to do. Shall I call for Mum and face Dad's wrath, or face the panda?

"Please, Maxine, I am not here to hurt you… I have a message for you," the panda spoke softly.

The loving tone of the panda's voice made my body uncurl. He gently sat beside me on my bed. Raising my head to meet his eyes, the fear faded, and curiosity started to take hold.

"What's the message?" I asked fearlessly.

For a split moment, his eyes look bigger, he looked sad.

"Some bad things are going to happen to you," he stared intensively into my eyes.

"What! What do you mean bad things are going to happen? Like what? Why me?" Panicked questions poured out of me.

I did not want anything bad to happen to me, I was a good girl, bad things only happened to naughty girls.

"What have I done wrong?" I asked, feeling confused and alarmed.

The panda placed his warm, gentle paw around my shoulder.

"Nothing… I am here to tell you that you are going to survive, you are going to be OK. I have to go now!"

"No, please don't leave me!" I pleaded.

I did not want the panda to leave me. I did not want him to go. I did not want to be alone; I did not want bad things to happen, and again fear tore through my small body.

The panda got up and strolled to my bedroom door.

"Please don't go!" I whispered to him.

He opened my door and walked along the shabby, narrow hallway, which contained two more doors and the exit to the stairway. Next to my door was my brother's room, and further down towards the stairs was the entrance to the forbidden room – Dad's room. The panda headed down the dark, shabby hallway. I tiptoed after him. The panda stopped outside my parents' bedroom. He slowly opened the door.

"No!" I exclaimed in a whisper!

The panda pushed the bedroom door open in a gentle manner and walked in. I gently crept after the bear, trying to miss the squeaky floorboard to avoid waking Dad. Tears were pouring down my face as I silently cried. Again, in a soft whisper, I begged him not to leave me.

The panda turned and faced me, and with one paw raised, he waved.

"Goodbye, Maxine," he gently whispered.

Suddenly he disappeared in front of me.

My heart sank; I felt sick; the tears continued to flow; I felt so alone and so afraid.

"What the hell are you doing in my f******g room?" Dad bellowed out!

The realisation hit me; I wanted the panda to stay so much that I had followed him into Dad's room, and I was now standing smack bang in the middle. As soon as the panda disappeared, my Dad woke up. Why couldn't he have woken up a few seconds earlier? He would have seen the bear. I gazed at his angry face and wanted to tell him I was not in his room to wake up Mum – I was not in the wrong. Tears suddenly dried up, and my breathing started to change, I began to hyperventilate.

For a moment, Dad's face softened, and he looked bewildered. He had not seen me like this before. However, he resumed his hard, angry face.

"Get out of my bedroom!" he bellowed.

I quickly ran like a timid little mouse scooting off to its den. I fled into my bedroom and jumped onto my bed, pulled the duvet up to my neck, and patiently waited for my punishment.

Suddenly my bedroom door flung open, and Dad came charging at me. I screwed up into a tight ball, my body so stiff, waiting for the blows. Nothing happened; I gingerly gazed up at him. He still had his hard, angry face.

"What have I told you?" he shouted in a stern voice.

"A panda bear has just visited me."

I followed him into your bedroom, where he disappeared," I blurted out in my defence.

My Dad's expression changed; he looked astonished. He knew deep down that I would never lie to him, it was not in my character to make up lies.

For the first time in my life, my dad was speechless. He always believed that there was life after death and believed in Angels and Demons.

He had a great interest in phenomena and things that could not be explained. He also believed that children could see more than adults due to their innocence. However, he paused for a moment, just staring at me, and then turned around and walked off.

The whole house was now awake, and my brother and I were allowed to venture downstairs, where we had to sit at the kitchen table and wait for breakfast. Dad was making tea while Mum was making breakfast.

Dad sat opposite me at the table, and Mum placed his breakfast in front of him. I had already finished my breakfast but was not allowed to leave the table until I was told. Dad picked up his knife and fork and tried to cut up the over-burnt sausage. He then gazed up at me.

"So, what did the panda bear have to say?"

Something told me not to tell him what the panda had said.

"He came to see me to check if I was okay and to say 'Hi.'"

Sadly, for me, the panda was right. A few weeks later, my mum got a new babysitter; he was in his late teens, and he was not nice, I took an instant dislike to him. For over a period of a year, he inflicted horrific and tortuous sexual acts on me that almost took my life. I kept this dark secret for many years. Turning forty and still having nightmares and trust issues, I took a huge step. I told Mum why the panda came to see me, she was devastated, and she fully supported my next decision. I went to the police and made a report, obviously leaving out the panda bear incident. Through the legal system, they put me in touch with a rape counsellor, and I had a significant result with the case. Hearing the panda's message rolling over in my mind, I know he was right, I had survived, and now I am going to be OK.

Running Bear told me this beautiful panda bear was an Angel who has transformed itself. He said to me if the Angel had transfigured into a Man or Woman, I would have called for my Mum and Dad. Coming as a bear was a less frightening figure for a small child to accept.

A note from your Angel

I am here standing right beside you, all you need to do is ask for my help.

Talk to me, tell me your concerns, and worries, your dreams and passions.

I will help you to get to your destination where you will feel happy and at peace with yourself.

One thing I would ask of you is, please stop hating yourself. You do not realise how magnificent and beautiful you are.

Here are some of my favourite crystals that will help you connect with your Angel. See if you can find one for yourself and sit and meditate with it. For a full explanation, please look at chapter

"Crystal Healing":

- Angelite – Angels – Spirit - Protection – Spiritual Growth
- Blue Kyanite – Trusting yourself – Psychic ability – Dreaming
- Caribbean Calcite – Communication with spirit
- Labradorite – Spiritual Growth – Magic – Trust in spirit
- Red Howlite – Emotions – Nurture relationships with females – Spiritual growth
- Serpentine – Spiritual Connection – Healing
- Sodalite – Spiritual Growth – Believe in yourself – Helps grief

Spirit Guides

Like Angels, we are born into this world with a Spirit Guide, we usually have one main one, but there may be up to several Guides at one time. These nonmain Guides come and go depending on your situation.

Becoming a new mother or father, you will have a new Guide coming into your life to help you with motherhood or fatherhood. These Guides are our teachers helping and guiding you. How do you know they are there? When a new one is coming in, you will feel all out of sorts for a few days, and when one is leaving, you will feel sad, as though you are missing someone for no reason, again, this will only last a few days.

Exercise 9 "Spirit Guides"

Take note in your journal of these feelings and ask yourself what is going on in your life.

Feeling all out of sorts – not too sure why?

Maybe this week, you start your driving lessons.

In this example, your main Guide has got you a new teacher to help you with your driving lessons.

Feeling sad, feels as though you are missing someone, but no one has left?

You have just finished your last exam, Yippee.

In this example, the Guide who helped you with your revision and exams has completed his task, he is no longer needed.

Your main Guide is your best friend, not everyone knows who their Guide is, I did not find out not to my late forties, but once I found out, everything in my life seemed to click, fall into place.

True Story: Running Bear

At a young age of seven years, I was fascinated and a bit obsessed with a song called "Running Bear" by Johnny Preston.

I would continually sing it all the time; I even wrote a story about it at school. I had a strong affinity to the Native American culture, and all my life, I heard whispers in my ears that I was a daughter of a shaman.

How did I find out? I went for a reading and was told by the medium that I had a Native American Indian man as my main Guide. As soon as she told me, I heard a voice inside my head, "Running Bear." The medium continued and said, "he's telling me his name is Running Bear." This was an extraordinary moment for me. Since then, we have grown strong together by meditating and trust.

One afternoon after doing meditation with him, I was sitting on the sofa, when I opened my eyes, I saw him sat right beside me. Yes, I did scream, not because I was frightened of him, it was because I am a jumpy soul. It was amazing seeing him. I have learned so much from Running Bear, mainly doing meditations with him, he told me when he had his human experience, he was a Shaman, and at the time, I was his daughter. Click, Click, my brain chinked.

I have Running Bear always beside me, guiding and helping me. The trust grew over time, even though there were times when I argued with him. I was asked out by a gentleman of similar age to me, we both decided to go for a coffee, I knew him via some neutral friends. Running Bear told me not to go, he is not for me. Yes, I am going, I argued back.

Running Bear just laughed. I met this man in the café shop, we sat at the table. OMG. The first thing he asked me if I was into football. If this is your thing, your passion, that is excellent, everyone is different, but it is not for me. So, I politely told him no. He knew that I worked for spirit, doing readings, healing, and teaching, etc. He told me he thought all of that was a load of rubbish and continued to babble on about football for an hour. During what seemed the most extended hour of my life, all I could hear was Running Bear laughing.

So, how do you know who your Guide is?

You may find you are drawn to someplace in the world or have a fascination with something. My friend is drawn to the Pharaohs of Egypt's times to discover one of the high priestesses was her Guide. My other friend was drawn to a forest, she was fascinated and particularly good with runes, and she had a way with the forestry animals to find out her Guide was a druid. In my example, I was drawn to the Native American culture.

Exercise 10 "Who is my Guide?"

Write down what you are drawn to in your journal, there may be a list, that is okay. Try some meditations, it may take time, so please be patient. Keep all your findings written down in your journal, you will notice a pattern forming. Ask yourself, do you feel a woman or male presence? The first thing that pops into your head is the answer, this is your Guide communicating with you. Keep asking questions, you can even ask for a name. I have known people to connect with their Guide first time only to doubt and dismiss everything. So, you need to have faith and belief.

Dreams are significant, this is the best way your guide and

loved ones in spirit can communicate with you. Write your vision down in your journal, you may not understand it now, but give it time to become a revelation. If you have any concerns or worries, it is good to ask for help from your Guide or Angel before sleep. In the morning, you will awake with ideas on how to help with your situation.

True Story: The Lions
When the children were young, I kept having a recurring nightmare for about a year. It terrified and tormented me, a group of lionesses and a huge male lion trying to attack and eat my children and me. I wanted to evaluate it and ask family and friends what it meant. They did not know and were all amused by this!

It was a beautiful day, the sun was out, and it was not too hot or cold. I walked through our local precinct, browsing the shop windows with my daughters Elisha, Paige, Brooke, Brodie, and son Jack. The town was not busy, and we were all happy as I promised them I would treat them to whatever they wanted. There was excitement and lots of laughter as we joked with each other.

As we approached one of the leading stores, suddenly, their doors flung open. People were flying out of doors, screaming.

Sheer fright was spread across their faces. We just paused as we could not believe what was happening. More and more people kept flooding out of the doors and running in all directions, yelling, and screaming. We could not make out what they were saying, the warm, happy feeling I had in my heart had now turned to pure fright. What was going on? My children drew close to me. I wished I had longer arms so I could hold them all.

An almighty scream, as though someone was being tortured,

came from inside the doorway.

Suddenly blood sprayed all over the window. There was a mighty roar. A big male lion leaped out of the doorway and landed in front of us, blood dripping from his big snarling fangs. Suddenly five more lionesses came charging out of the door. One of them had torn off a human arm and held it in her mouth as though it was a trophy. These lions were not hunting for food, they were hunting to kill. There they were all in front of us, and we were next!

Adrenaline pumped through my body as one voice screamed through my brain.

"Get the children to safety."

I whisked Jack up in my arms as he was the youngest. I then grabbed Brodie's hand as she was the next smallest and screamed to my other children to run into the nearest doorway, which was only a few metres away! Running as fast as I could with the lions on our heels, we managed to get to the door. As I threw Brodie and Jack into the shop, the male lion leaped on me…

I woke up in a sweat… Another dream about these lions, but in a different location. I am always with my children, and the children's safety is the scariest part as I know if I fail, the lions will get them.

A mother's nightmare! I was getting to a point where these dreams were becoming a concern as I did not understand why I was always getting them.

So, one night before going to bed, I ask my Guide to give me an answer.

I was in a posh restaurant, and I was sitting at a well laid-out table.

There was a bottle of champagne on ice.

Sitting opposite me was Steve, a well-groomed man I had been romantically involved with for the last eighteen months. Things had not been going well between us, and I had tried numerous times to break it off.

"Maxine, we have a whole week where it's just you and me… no kids, just us!" he announced firmly.

I realised we must be on holiday. I felt like I was choking as the restaurant's walls closed in on me, squeezing the air out of my lungs. I politely told him that I was going to the ladies and excused myself.

I had no intention of going there, I just wanted to get out! To my relief, my car was parked straight outside with the motor running. It was as though it knew that I wanted to get away. I jumped into my reliable vehicle and drove off as fast as I could. I had no idea where I was, but I did not seem to care, my only concern was to get away quickly and as far as possible. I was driving on a straight road, something like you see in America… a long straight highway out in the desert. I kept driving and driving. Dusk was settling in; the straight road ahead was coming to an end. As I slowed up, a church was on the left-hand side with lots of cars parked outside. I noticed people pouring out of the church doors. I pulled up to the church and parked. Getting out of the car, I felt a strange sensation as though I was magnetically drawn to something or someone.

I made my way up the steps and into the church hall. There were more people inside getting ready to go. I had caught the end of a service. As I gazed around, I noticed a middle-aged man, smartly dressed in a navy suit, heading towards me.

"Maxine, I have been waiting for you."

I was shocked and taken aback, he knew me. The man gazed at my bedazzled face and smiled, he explained he was a medium who had just conducted a service.

"Maxine, I have a message for you!"

"Me?" I gasped, still feeling dazed.

"The male lion… is… Steve!"

I woke up, bolted upright in my bed, the penny dropped. It was so clear and so obvious; the lion was Steve.

For the last several months, he had been abusively pressuring me. He demanded we ought to marry, to move in with me, wanted me to support him financially, and wanted children. The more I kept saying no to him, the more he applied the pressure and began to verbally abuse me. He repeatedly told me I was useless at everything and that I ought to be thankful for him as he was brilliant. As a single mum raising five children, this guy threatened my existence – hence the nightmares. I was trying to fight for the survival of my children and myself.

Coming to a realisation, I knew what I had to do. By the end of the day, I was no longer seeing Steve. Since that day, the nightmares of the lions have stopped!

Connecting with your Guide through dreams is extremely powerful. Running Bear helped me through this challenging time and made me realise what I needed to do for my children and me.

The difference between your Guide and your Angel is that even though they are helping and guiding you, Angels can intervene in your life by performing miracles, whereas your Guide cannot. Your Guide can ask for intervention via your Angel. There are rules in the spirit world, I know there was a time Running Bear got into trouble. There was no punishment, the Angels told him he could not do that again.

True Story: Punched

I was thirty-six weeks heavily pregnant, I had giant babies, and the more I had, the bigger they got.

At the time, I was carrying my youngest child, Jack. I had four other children, Brodie was only turning ten months old, Brooke just coming up to two years, Paige was five years old, and Elisha was seven. As you can imagine, I had my hands full.

Brodie was a fussy eater, she would only have Heinz baby food, porridge, egg custard, and rice pudding, she refused to eat anything else. This day, I went shopping for Brodie's food. I had to bulk buy just in case the shops ran out. I left my husband at home to look after the children. I was not gone long, but when I returned home, the house was in chaos. All my children crying while my husband was screaming and shouting at them. I quickly put the shopping bags onto the kitchen sides and went to console my children while my husband went outside into the back garden to light up a cigarette. Once the children calmed down and were happy, I went to the kitchen to pop away the food. I was furious with him, but I tried to calm myself. (I had high blood pressure, and if I could not get it down, my doctor was going to put me into the hospital). My husband came through the back door and stood quietly beside me; I was just going to pack away Brodie's food when he snatched the bag out of my hands. He burst into a violent rage and started to smash the baby food onto the side counter. I stood there while he hurled abuse at me. When he finished, he threw the bag on the floor and stood glaring at me. I felt vulnerable and scared for my baby, I knew what he was like. Was he going to punch me in the stomach? Suddenly, he was on the ground, unconscious. I was looking at my right fist. Did I hit him? I had no intention to. I felt as though someone had taken over my right arm. It was not me who knocked him to the floor.

I know now it was Running Bear, I disagree with violence, but on this occasion, I thanked my Guide for his help. So, the rule is that your Guide cannot intervene in your life, but sometimes they can take over your arm and punch someone in the face. Lol.

Start today, connect, bond with your Guide, but more importantly, believe in the voice in your head, especially if it is pushing you out of your comfort zone.

Exercise 11 "Communicate with your Guides"

This simple meditation technique is an extremely excellent way to let your Guides communicate with you. You can meditate for one minute, five minutes, or however long you want. This is the meditation I had been doing, and after several times of doing it, Running Bear materialised right beside me.

Many people tend to find it hard to meditate as constant thoughts randomly interrupt their peace. They are trying too hard to concentrate on nothing and find it annoying when reminded that they are out of milk or sugar. This is the monkey brain that chitters and chatters, so all you need to do is quieten it.

To quieten the monkey brain, all you need to do is give it a task, such as telling it to concentrate on breathing.

Breathe in… Breathe out…
Breathe in… Breathe out…
Breathe in… Breathe out…

Just simply be aware of your breath.

Thoughts from the back of your head will come to the forefront, you may see flashing colours, feel a sense of warmth, and feel a whisper in your ear. This is spirit and your Guide coming forth. If you can do this meditation at least once a day, you will have some incredible experiences and write down your experience in your journal.

A note from your Spirit Guide

I am communicating in many ways.

We will find a method of communication that is special to us.
Keep up the good work, keep believing, as I feel our bond is getting stronger.

Here are some of my favourite crystals that will help you connect with your Guide. See if you can find one for yourself and sit and meditate with it. For a full explanation, please look at chapter "Crystal Healing":

➤ Angelite – Angels – Spirit– Protection – Spiritual Growth

➤ Blue Kyanite – Trusting yourself – Psychic ability – Dreaming

➤ Caribbean Calcite – Communication with spirit

➤ Labradorite – Spiritual Growth – Magic – Trust in spirit

➤ Red Howlite – Emotions – Nurture relationships with females – Spiritual growth

➤ Serpentine – Spiritual Connection – Healing

➤ Sodalite – Spiritual Growth – Believe in yourself – Helps grief

Loved Ones in Spirit

Losing a loved one, a mother, father, daughter, son, partner, etc., is a devastating and traumatic time. Even when we know they are dying, for an instant, my father was only given six months to live, he had been diagnosed with lung cancer. It was like watching a strong, healthy father deteriorating into a skeleton of a man, and there was nothing I could do about it. Feeling inadequate, hopeless, and hating the illness taking over my father's life fuelled the darkness inside me, mentally punishing and tormenting myself. Putting a lid on these cruel feelings, squashing it deep within my soul, as I had to put on a brave face for my father, I unknowingly allowed them to fester. What I should have done at the time was to show myself kindness, treat myself as a dear friend. This is not a selfish act, and you, my friend, if you find yourself in a similar position, you must do the same, speak out and be kind to yourself.

The only peace I had when my father passed is that I knew he would always be in my life. I knew death was just a passing, a time to go home. His funeral was more of a celebration of his life on earth, and even though I missed him in the physical sense, he still, to this day, pops back to see me.

A poem based on Henry Scott-Holland that was read at my father's funeral.

Death is nothing at all.
I have only slipped away into the next room.

I am I, and you are you.
Whatever we were to each other, that we are still.

Call me by the old familiar name.
Speak of me in the easy way which you always used.
Put no difference into your tone.
Wear no forced air of solemnity of sorrow.

Laugh as we always laughed at the little jokes that we enjoyed together.
Play, smile, think of me, pray for me.
Let my name be ever the household word that it always was.
Let it be spoke without an effort, without the ghost of a shadow on it.

Life means all that it ever meant.
It is the same as it ever was.
There is absolute and unbroken continuity.

Why should I be out of mind because I am out of sight?
I am but waiting for you, for an interval.
Somewhere extremely near.
Just around the corner.

All is well.

True Story: Dad
I had only been divorced a few years when a friend introduced me to a nice gentleman at one of her dinner parties. Tim seemed a polite and quiet man who kindly asked me if I would like to go out to dinner with him. He told me he knew an excellent

restaurant situated in the New Forest. I felt brave and accepted his kind offer. This feeling of bravery did not last long on the actual day I was kicking myself. Why did I agree? I was a complete nervous wreck, I had not been out for ages, let alone going out for a date. My wardrobe looked as though a hurricane had torn through it as I tossed each garment aside.

What was I going to wear?

In my sheer panic, I suddenly felt as though I had been hit by lightning. Oh my god! What should I say if he asks me…? My whole life revolved around spirit. At present, I was designing my own tarot cards, and each month I sold my spiritual artwork at a local artist's market, I worked part-time doing readings over the telephone. I was involved in running psychic fairs and doing more readings. I went to a closed circle a couple of times a week and started to venture out on the platform, but…a big but… what do I say about the ghostly visitors that come to see me? Oh no! Making a snap decision, I knew that I could not mention any of this to him, otherwise, he would think that I was completely insane!

It was a dark, cold evening, Tim was prompt collecting me.

Feeling intensely nervous, I kept quiet.

Tim seemed to come out of his shell, and I found him loud and bold. He loved talking boastfully about his achievements in life… which was perfect. I just sat in the passenger side of his car, praying he would not shut up.

I was sitting in the car for at least twenty minutes, staring out into the cold dark night. Tim was still droning on, by which point I had completely switched off.

I noticed the bright lights ahead and heard the crunch of gravel underneath the tyres, the car was slowly coming to a stop. I got out into the sharp, fresh air and gasped as I gazed up at the magnificent medieval building, which had been converted into a stylish restaurant.

Walking into the reception, I was extremely impressed by the architecture, which combined the old with the new. A young, friendly lady greeted us and showed us to our table, situated in a glamorous conservatory. I could not believe how quiet it was, we had the place to ourselves. Taking my seat, I could not help noticing how pitch dark it was outside, which made all the windows become like black mirrors. I caught my reflection and quickly tucked my protruding curl behind my ear.

Ordering from the menu, Tim continued with his nonstop talkfest, now whinging about his failed marriage. I was so looking forward to my food, in my sheer panic and anxiety attack, I had forgotten to eat anything, and my growling stomach was a constant reminder.

I noticed on the menu they had my favourite – hot chocolate fudge cake with fresh cream.

My small stomach cannot contain a three-course meal, so I just ordered a main meal to look forward to my pudding.

Sitting opposite Tim, I suddenly felt a shiver run up my spine, I felt icy coldness on my body's right side. I could feel my hair moving as though someone was running their fingers gently through it.

Oh no, I screamed silently as I caught my reflection in the mirror. There was no visible sign of anyone standing beside me.

Suddenly I had flashing thoughts, I could clearly see a young maid, dressed shabbily in a long grey dress with a white doyley hat, with all her hair neatly tucked into it.

I felt her excitement as she knew that I could sense her.

Trying to ignore her, telling her to go away in my mind, I could feel her touching my face.

It felt like I walked into cobwebs, which were tickling and making my nose twitch. Trying to stay composed, not wanting to give the game away, I repeatedly told her to go.

The main meal arrived, and throughout the duration, the little minx would not leave me alone. Once I finished my lovely meal, I excused myself and told Tim I needed to powder my nose.

The toilet was small and quaint, only housing three cubicles. As I came out of the cubicle and stood at the basin, washing my hands, I could feel she was with me. I had told her numerous times that I just wanted to be left alone, I did not want to speak to her, why wouldn't she just leave me alone?

"For god's sake, I've told you! I don't want to speak to you!" I found myself shouting in the quiet restroom.

Suddenly all three doors on the cubicles started to violently slam simultaneously. For a split second, I looked around to see if any windows were open, I thought it was a freaky gust of wind or something.

There were no windows, no drafts, I felt immense anger burning through the atmosphere as all three doors continued to freakily slam. Feeling very frightened, I fled and returned to the table.

Tim did not even notice how stressed I looked, all I wanted was to get out of the building, I just wanted to go home.

"Do you want pudding?" The first and only question he asked me.

"No thanks... in fact... I am not feeling very well... do you mind? Could you take me home?"

"Well, I'm here now, I want pudding. You will have to wait," he announced obnoxiously.

What an idiot. Feeling trapped and terrified, I could feel myself shaking. I completely blanked him as he started up the boring lecture about his life. I was so worried and so frightened; I knew the angry spirit would return. I refused to have a pudding, hoping it would put him off having one, but he took great delight in eating his in front of me.

Any minute she will be here.

Glancing down at the table, I closed my eyes and prayed, I asked my Spiritual Family to help me, please protect me.

Opening my eyes, I saw a reflection of a man dressed in a smart navy suit, he looked as though he was in his early thirties. Squeezing my eyes, I noticed he had dark jet-black hair, there was something familiar about his features, but he was too far away to acknowledge him. Glancing over my shoulder to get a better look, I was shocked to find no one was there.

When I glanced back at the window, he was still there. I felt a wave of warmth and love, I knew this gentle spirit did not mean any harm, I felt slightly relaxing. Was he there protecting me? He stayed with me throughout the painful meal. I never once felt the presence of the other angry spirit. When it was time to go, I saw him vanish. On the way home, completely ignoring Tim, I stared out into the cold dark night and thanked my Spiritual Family and the kind spirit for his help.

Once I got home, I sent Tim packing, never seeing him again.

I could not believe my eyes as I walked into the living room, the girls had been going through some old photographs.

"Mum, look!" Elisha shoved a photograph in my hand.

It was a picture of a man with jet black hair in his early thirties dressed in a smart navy suit.

"Dad!" I gasped.

Our loved ones that have returned home are always in our life.

Talk to them as they are still here, they love to hear your words and your voice. If you are worried or need advice, they will help. They will give you signs that they are there. You may feel them softly stroking your face as your drift off to sleep, you may feel them sitting down beside you on the sofa. They can give you so many signs, take notes, and write these special moments in your journal.

True Story: Nan Sort Them Out
Many years ago, one evening, as per usual, I sent the three younger children up to bed.

"Come on, upstairs, and clean your teeth, don't forget to wash and then get into bed."

I was sitting in the living room, trying to have a conversation with my eldest daughter.

Brooke and Brodie were eight and nine years old at the time and shared a bedroom. This night they misbehaved; they were hyper! They did not brush their teeth or have a wash, as they were too busy playing around.

After several attempts at shouting up the stairs and telling them to get into bed, I started to get annoyed! Finally, I snapped, I called both downstairs. They stood in front of me, trying not to nudge each other and giggle.

Suddenly I could smell the musk perfume – a fragrance that only Nan wore. Knowing she was near; I could not help myself.

"Look, if you don't go to bed, I'll get my Nan to sort you out!" Both children just looked at me, totally confused.

"But your Nan is dead, what is she going to do?" asked Brooke in disbelief.

"Right, go to bed and be quiet!" I snapped.

The two mischievous children walked up to their rooms,

continuing to giggle away at each other.

"Sort them out, Nan," I whispered.

I continued my conversation with Elisha, within three minutes, we heard almighty screams coming from their bedroom. I launched out of my chair and raced into the hallway. Brooke and Brodie came charging down the stairs towards me, screaming in sheer fright, they both flung their arms around me tightly. Tears poured down their faces.

"What's up? What's happened?" I asked anxiously.

When they had gone back to their bedroom, they thought I was crazy, what can a ghost do?

Ignoring my warning, they continued playing their games. In their bedroom, they had a small alcove, which I had made into a wardrobe. Instead of putting a door on the front, I had made a pull-back curtain that they could quickly move to get to their clothes. As they were playing, a bright light had suddenly appeared behind the curtain.

They both looked at each other puzzled.

"Where has that light come from?" Brodie had wondered.

"There isn't a light in the wardrobe," Brooke had replied.

They both went over to pull back the curtain. There in front of them was a massive orb. It floated towards them! They both screamed and ran.

"I told you I would get my Nan to sort you out!" I laughed.

"Please send her away, please, please, please tell her we'll be good…we promise to go to bed," pleaded Brodie.

"OK." I smiled.

After that, they both went to bed, and guess what! Not one peep from the pair of them!

I can tell you many stories about my beloved Dad, Nan, and Grandad. I have been blessed with so many incredible spiritual experiences during my dark times, helping and uplifting my soul. Your family is doing the same, just believe and talk to them.

You may already have been getting signs that they are around you. Embrace these beautiful experiences, notice their timing is perfect. When I feel low, I find them more active, letting me know they are there for me.

My beautiful Spiritual Family helps me, but there have also been times when a beloved pet returned.

True Story: Jack
At the time, all the children were relatively young. Jack was only eight months old and crawling; Brodie was one and half years old and full of mischief; Brooke was two years old and immensely proud that she was not wearing nappies any more. Paige was coming up to five years old and just started school. Elisha, the eldest, was eight years old and a big help. At the time, my abusive husband had got a promotion at work, which meant he had to work away permanently. It was heaven... blissful, no more tension, no more walking around on eggshells, and no more abuse. Believe it or not, peace and harmony and so much laughter echoed through the house.

Being an over-protective mother, I made sure their loving environment was child-proof, removing sharp corners, putting safety plugs into the plug sockets, locks on lower kitchen cabinets, and most importantly, a fitted secure stair gate.

One evening as per usual, I quickly popped into the kitchen to make everyone a drink. Brodie was sat in her bouncing chair; Brooke, Paige, and Elisha were all sitting on the settee watching cartoons on the TV. Jack was happy and content playing on his activity mat. Before leaving the room, I asked Elisha to keep an eye on him.

I was only going to be a few minutes.

Standing at the kitchen table, I quickly got their cups and bottle and put them on the side; suddenly, I heard a man calling my name.

"Maxine!"

Dropping everything, I darted to the front door. I stood still and looked around. There was no one there.

"Maxine!" I heard the man shout again.

I gasped as I suddenly realised who was calling my name.

"Granddad?"

"Jack!" he shouted.

I immediately rushed to the living room.

I hastily scanned around the room, but I could not see him; my heart jumped up into my mouth as panic set in.

Suddenly I could hear a giggle behind me.

I spun around and rushed to the foot of the stairs. I gasped with shock and horror. The stair gate was wide open, and Jake was two stairs away from the top, looking very unsteady; he was going to fall. Automatically, I raced up the stairs. I just got to him in time as Jack fell back, catching him in my arms; Jack found it all amusing. Holding him tightly in my arms as he giggled, I could feel my heart pounding. I carried him down the stairs and, after securing the gate, I needed to sit down.

"Thank you, Granddad."

True Story: Caught You Out

Shortly after my divorce, I plucked up the courage to start dating, I had been seeing a guy called Sean for several weeks. He was only a couple of years older than me and was a manager of a successful company. He had never married nor had kids. He told me he had never met the right woman.

He was a very spiritual man and believed in the same concepts as me; he too had seen ghosts and believed there was more to life than just the rat race. At the start of the relationship, I was honest and upfront with him. I placed all my cards on the table and told him I did not want to rush into anything serious and that I needed time. He came across as very understanding and supportive, which was a rare experience for me.

Every Thursday night, I went to an evening class to train as a reflexologist. Afterward, I went and met him at his local pub for a quick drink. His dad drank there, and he would often join us for a drink. He was a man in his late eighties. He was a remarkably warm, friendly man who went to the gym five times a week and was as fit as a fiddle.

He, too, was very spiritual, and he took a great interest in the course I was doing.

One Thursday evening, we were sitting in the pub with his dad Pete and a few of Sean's friends. Sean was interested in talking to his mates about football while talking to his dad about what I had learned that evening.

Suddenly a man whispered in my ear; turning around, there was no one behind me. Stunned and shocked, I recognised the voice… Dad!

"Sean took a woman out for a drink this Tuesday."

I could not help myself, I just blurted it out.

"You took a woman out this Tuesday for a drink," I accused Sean.

He was startled and taken aback at my intrusive behaviour. The table went quiet, all eyes were fixed on him, all waiting for his reply.

"Don't be stupid, I didn't take anyone out… I'm not interested in anyone but you!"

"OK."

I felt silly at my sudden outburst. I felt my cheeks burning with embarrassment as they all laughed at me, except for Pete.

"What made you say that?"

Looking at him, I did not want to sound mad, but something inside told me he would not judge me in that way.

"My dad whispered it to me."

"Really, wow, that's amazing!"

Suddenly it happened again.

"He took her to the Pilgrim pub in Matchwood!"

Where? I had never heard of this pub, and my geographical knowledge of Matchwood was non-existent. I had the urge again to blurt it out.

"You took her to the Pilgrim pub in Matchwood!" This time I was adamant I was not going crazy.

As I said it, he was in the process of taking a sip of his beer; hearing the accusation, he choked on it. Gagging and coughing, his face went bright red with fury.

"Who told you that? I never took anyone out!" he shouted at me.

I remained quiet and still as he ranted and raved, but he was only digging a grave for himself. He suddenly turned his fury onto his mates, accusing them of stitching him up. He wanted to know which one had told me; obviously, they all denied the accusation, which frustrated him even more.

"Who told you?" he demanded.

I did not say a word and remained calm, but I had had a real eye-opener to find out what he was really like. I continued to just stare at him.

"Look, it was nothing… she's a friend … I work with her; she is going through a bad divorce… you know what it is like? I just took her out for a friendly drink… that was all!" He tried to reason.

"So, when did you take her out?" I spoke softly.

"This Tuesday." He lowered his head.

"Where did you take her?"

"To the Pilgrim pub in Matchwood," he whispered, hoping no one would hear him.

There were gasps around the table, followed by an awkward silence.

"Who told you?" He lifted his head.

"My dad!" I glared at him.

"But he's d…!" Fear tore across his face.

Not raising my voice, I gathered my belongings and said my goodbyes to everyone. That was the last I saw of him.

True Story: My Daughter

It was a rare day – all the children were at school, Elisha was at college, and, for once in a long time, I had the day off, so I thought it would be an excellent opportunity to catch up on some of the housework.

I was in the living room polishing the sideboard. I placed the remote control for the television neatly on the side, and suddenly I heard someone running down the stairs and jumping onto the landing floor. Spinning around, startled, I could not believe my eyes – a girl a couple years younger than Elisha, who was the spitting image of her. She had the same-coloured blonde shoulder-length hair, and ran past the living room door heading towards the kitchen. Dropping the duster, I quickly darted out of the room. I looked frantically around the kitchen, but there was no one there. The back door was securely locked, where was she? A sudden warm realisation overwhelmed me; I had tears welling up in my eyes. Thirteen years ago, I was six months pregnant and went into early labour. It was a horrific and devastating time, and my baby girl had died.

I returned to the living room and sat down. A tear rolled down my cheek; what a wonderful experience to know that my little girl was close by. Jumping to my feet, I continued to clean, keeping this special moment to myself.

Unexpectedly, Elisha arrived home earlier than usual; she told me there was an event taking place involving all the teachers, which meant the students could go home. I was standing at the kitchen sink, giving it a good clean as Elisha told me about her day. I never once mentioned the magical moment that I experienced earlier.

"Is it okay to watch a bit of TV, Mum?"

"Yeah… sure."

After a few minutes, Elisha came rushing into the kitchen.

"Mum! Mum!"

Turning around, I was stunned at what Elisha had to say. She told me she went to get the remote control from the sideboard when she heard someone running down the stairs and jumping onto the landing floor. Spinning around, she saw a blonde-haired girl who looked like her running past the door heading towards the kitchen.

As you can imagine, my jaw hit the floor. What a wonderful experience we both shared.

True Story: Betsie

I had a little black and white cat called Betsie, who I dearly loved. Going to bed each night, I had to leave my right foot out of the covers as she would curl up around my foot and sleep with me for the night.

Sometimes it was a bit unpleasant, especially if it were raining, she would come in drench and cuddle my foot tightly to warm herself up. Things we must endure for our animal… lol. Sadly, Betsie died, she was knockdown by a car.

I was devasted and missed her dearly.

Going to bed one night, I was still in the habit of leaving my right foot exposed, drifting off to sleep, I was woken. I could feel Betsie curling her little body around my foot. I smiled to myself and then panic as I realised Betsie was dead. Bolting upright in bed, looking down at my foot, there was nothing there. To this day, I keep my foot out of the covers, and on some occasions, I can feel Betsie cuddling my foot.

Remember, the ones you have lost, whether it was a beloved mother or cat, are always with us. Talk to them, and watch out for the signs, here are some: you can smell their fragrance, smoke if they were a little chimney, you suddenly go cold and feel shivers going up your spine. Your keys disappearing and turning up in an unusual place. Their picture being repositioned, and your TV is unexpectedly being turned off. They can manifest themselves so you can clearly see them, but this takes a lot of their energy and can be quite tricky. The best way to see your loved ones, is your peripheral vision, as soon as you turn your head towards them, they will disappear. It is to do with the lenses of your eye not completely cover the edges. The trick is to continue to look forwards, and you will be able to see them clearly in your peripheral.

Just a little note to say, if you have not been experiencing any of the above, just reading this book will ignite your spiritual awakening.

Do not be afraid, your beautiful Spiritual Family loves you

and wants the best for you. Ask them for their help, guidance, or just have a little natter with them like you use to do.

A note from your Love Ones in Spirit

I am here and have not gone away, I walk beside you every day.

You are loved and cherished, you are beautiful like a bright shining star.

Talk to me like we once used to, and I will show you signs that I am there for you.

I love you with my whole being and so proud of you.

Keep your chin up and keep moving forwards, remember you are never on your own.

Here are some of my favourite crystals that will help you connect with your loved ones in spirit. See if you can find one for yourself and sit and meditate with it. For a full explanation, please look at chapter "Crystal Healing":

➤ Angelite – Angels – Spirit – Protection – Spiritual Growth

➤ Blue Kyanite – Trusting yourself – Psychic ability – Dreaming

➤ Caribbean Calcite – Communication with spirit

➤ Labradorite – Spiritual Growth – Magic – Trust in spirit

➤ Red Howlite – Emotions – Nurture relationships with females – Spiritual growth

➤ Serpentine – Spiritual Connection – Healing

➤ Sodalite – Spiritual Growth – Believe in yourself – Helps grief

Animal Spirit

What are Animal Spirits? Like Guides and Angels, everyone has an animal spirit with them, there can be several, but you always have one main one. They give us strength and courage in our darkest hour.

True Story: Tiger
I run as fast as I can, my heart is beating hard in my chest, fear races through my body, I must escape. My legs are beginning to fatigue.

"Ouch!" I cry as a tree branch whips my face.

I stumble and trip over a tree stump, falling onto the soggy yellow and brown leaves that carpet the woodland floor. I gaze up at the bare trees surrounding me, puffing, and panting, I can see the hotness of my breath steaming in the icy air. It is cold and getting dark. I must get up, I must get away, I must get to safety. Standing on my feet, I can feel a sharp pain in my left ankle. As darkness drawls in, the trees around me take on a haunting silhouette.

Frantically gazing around me, I toss and turn my head. I felt confused, but I am so scared that I do not know which way I should go.

I am lost, I am alone, and I am terrified. I gaze up at the silvery full moon that shines so fiercely in the navy sky, I hope it will give me a sign or a direction.

Suddenly, there again, I hear a loud howling noise. My heart almost bursts out of my chest in fear as the sound seems to close in on me. Trying to run but finding it difficult due to my painful ankle, I frantically hobble, furiously trying to get away as the darkness of the woods makes me its blinded prisoner. I start frantically feeling the trees with my palms, I am so desperate to escape.

Again, suddenly I hear another loud howling noise, but this time, it seems much closer.

Picking up speed, smacking my sore bloody hands harder and faster around the sharp knobbly trees, being whipped by unsuspecting branches, I move forward hastily. My pounding heart beating loudly, I must get away, I must get out.

I gasp in fright; I can feel the hair on the back of my neck stand up as I sense the vibrations and the hotness of the predator's breath. I know it is standing right behind me, I hear it growling and snarling.

My whole-body trembles with fright as I feel it is going to tear me to shreds. As I stand frozen to the spot in sheer terror, waiting for it to pounce on me, I notice something moving towards me.

Trying hard to focus my night vision, I am stunned and curious as something big and fast rumbles through the nestled shrubs' thickness. I am amazed as it gets closer, and I can see it glowing with magnificent sparkling colours. The fear trembling through my body starts to evaporate as curiosity starts to take hold. I can clearly see something hurrying towards me…

Standing in front of me is the most glorious, beautiful creature that I have ever seen – a big, beautiful, orange tiger with a white glowing aura surrounding him and sparkling colours glittering around him – he stands and stares at me. A strange feeling takes hold of my body, but I do not fear him. I feel as though he is charging me up with so much strength and courage. The energy surging through my body is so powerful that it makes me feel invincible.

Suddenly, I turn and face the snarling creature standing behind me. It is tall and big; it looks like a big black wolf standing on its hind legs.

It has big teeth, razor-sharp claws, and red, fierce eyes. With the magnificent, powerful tiger by my side, we both launched ourselves at the werewolf and tear it to shreds in a synchronising movement.

"Maxine, Maxine, wake up, you have to get ready for school!" Mum shouted as she stood by my bedroom door.

After being so violently and sexually abused at the age of six, I started to have terrible night terrors every night. I always dreamt that some form of monster wanted to either torture or kill me, but whenever I felt hopeless, this amazing tiger would appear and would give me the strength and courage to face my fear and destroy it.

At the age of ten, I mastered the art of keeping my nightmares a secret. Mum and Dad would often visit a spiritualist church, they attended a service that was held on a Sunday evening.

One Sunday evening, Dad took me along with him. I had never attended a spiritualist church, I was somewhat nervous, I did not know what to expect, but I felt excitement bubbling up in my stomach.

Walking towards the church holding Dad's hand, it was dark and cold. We were both wearing our warm, thick coats and scarves around our necks.

The church was situated in the middle of a row of houses, it was a small building with a pitch-point roof. The highest point of the church housed a lit cross that shone brightly in the dark.

Another warm light seeped from the slightly open double front doors. Dad opened one of the doors, and I stepped into a brightly lit, warm lobby.

Dad closed the front door behind us.

In front of me was another thick door. I tried to force the door open with all my might, only to be swept back by its heaviness. Dad laughed at my poor attempt, and with one big strong arm, he opened the door effortlessly. Stepping through the door, we found an elderly man and lady standing in front of us.

The elderly man, who must have been in his late sixties, was dressed in a three-piece, brown tweed suit; he was bald on top of his head with thin, grey, short hair rimming from one ear to the other. I noticed that he had a huge nose and big ears with white hair sprouting out of them, both features looked out of proportion with his small head. Even though he had a hard, leathery face, he had a warm, kind smile.

Standing beside him was a glamorous elderly lady, she must have been in her late sixties, but she looked so much younger than her companion. She wore a pretty, long, pleated, lilac skirt with a white blouse neatly tucked in, showing off her plump figure, and had a sparkly, purple necklace floating around her neck. She had big, white, puffy hair that was immaculately in place. With her bright purple lipstick, she, too, beamed a kind, warm smile.

In her hands, she was holding several hymn books. When she saw me entering through the doorway, she greeted me with her friendly smile and handed one to me. I quickly turned around and glanced at Dad for his permission.

"It's OK, take it," he consented.

As I stepped forward towards the lady to take the book, the elderly man suddenly took a huge step back from me and held up his hands as though I was pointing a gun at him.

"Wow, that's a big tiger you have with you, young lady!" he bellowed out.

I just stood there staring at him in bewilderment and shock.

"Do you know you have a big tiger with you?" he asked.

I remained quiet as thoughts raced through my mind, how did he know about my tiger?

"Yes, Maxine has a thing about tigers," Dad interrupted the silence, saving me.

"Argh, does she now?" the man gave me a knowing look.

Dad gave a small laugh as he quickly reminisced.

"Yeah, her first-ever word was tiger... it's strange, though... no one ever taught her that word," he said thoughtfully.

"Really," again, the elderly man said intentionally.

"Yeah, at an early age, she told my wife and me that she could see a tiger.

At the age of three, my wife and I bought her a kitten, Maxine picked the kitten with the stripes and had to call him Tiger. She was so devoted and caring for that cat!"

Both men laughed, and both gave me a loving look while I stood patiently and quietly, feeling somewhat uncomfortable as they continued to talk about me. The elderly lady greeted everyone who came through the door and handed them a hymn book.

"The funny thing is, that we all thought Tiger was a Tom until he had a bunch of kittens, so we had to name her Tiger Lil!" Again, both men found this amusing as they both let out a small laugh.

Dad continued the conversation with the elderly man, who seemed extremely interested in what he had to say, listening attentively to his every word, and giving him nods and smiles in the appropriate places. He was fascinated.

"I tell you what, though… when Tiger Lil had her kittens, she had them in the coal bunker outside in the garden. Pearl, my wife, made up a box for them and wanted to put them underneath the stairs to keep them warm and safe, but when she went to bring the kittens inside, Tiger Lil went for her. She was like a wild cat and scratched Pearl's hand… quite badly… so she asked me if I could fetch them in… Oh my god! I had never seen Tiger Lil behave like it. She went mad at me too. There was no way that I could get close to her kittens. At the time, Maxine was coming up to four years old. When we told her Tiger was not a boy as she had had a litter of kittens, she was over the moon.

"Do you know what?"

"Maxine went to the coal bunker, and Tiger Lil let her bring the kittens in… Maxine was the only one allowed to touch her kittens."

"It was amazing!"

I felt somewhat embarrassed, listening to Dad bragging about me, but the elderly man looked down and gave me a meaningful smile.

"You know your animal spirit is a big tiger!"

This was not the last time I heard this. Throughout my life, I have come across so many spiritual people who have randomly told me the same thing, I can feel his presence all the time.

The most memorable and meaningful time was when Dad had only a few weeks to live. He told me he could see so many wonderful spiritual things, he was not scared of death.

He told me to look in his art book, he was an amazing artist, he had something for me. Opening his book, I could not believe it, it was so breath-taking… I could feel myself welling up.

"I've drawn this for you… This is what your tiger looks like… I can see him standing right beside you!"

How to find out who is your animal spirit, is simple. What animal do you adore the most? I loved tigers from such an early age, and I was also drawn to wolves. I grew up with German Shepard dogs and had the pleasure of having them in my adult life.

Running Bear did a life regression with me during a meditation, where he took me back to the time when I was an Indian Maiden, I must admit I have never felt so free and happy.

I discovered I had a big black wolf with me, I rescued him as a puppy and raised him as one of my own.

His name was Shadow, everywhere I went, he followed. Finding this out was remarkable for me, it inspired me to create a Wolf Oracle Cards. Your animal spirit can inspire you to do something creative or something extraordinary.

Exercise 12 "Who is my Animal Spirit?"
Write down in your journal what animal do you love the most? Then do a meditation with your guide, or you can do a guided meditation with Jason Stephenson, "meet your animal spirit" on YouTube. Again, write down in your journal your discoveries.

True Story: Power of your Animal Spirit
You can call upon your animal spirit to protect you. There was a man named John who liked going to his local pub for a couple of drinks. He believed in Spirit and knew he had a giant grizzly bear that walked with him. He was a kind and gentleman, he was not the type to look for trouble, he liked the simple life. One night at

141

the pub, some travellers were drinking in there, causing chaos. He finished his pint and thought it would be best to head off home. When he got outside, all the travellers followed him out.

They surrounded him, and it was apparent they wanted to hurt him. John told them to let him go, he did not want any trouble, but this seemed to egg them on. John stood silently and took a deep breath, he called upon his giant grizzly bear. The men around him started to scream in fear as a ball of energy cover John's body, which morphed into his bear. These men fled and never returned to the pub ever again.

True Story: Silverback Gorilla

A good friend of mine, Sue, works in the evening and finishes around ten p.m. In the winter months walking home, it is quite eerie and dark. On her way home, she must walk past a small woodland that sits in front of her house. Walking along the short pathway to her home, she feels very vulnerable and scared. The woods are known for their junkies and other unsavoury characters. At any moment, anyone could grab her and drag her off.

A year ago, Sue found out she has an enormous silverback gorilla with her. Every time Sue finishes work, she calls upon him for protection. Sue is a petite lady, but she can feel herself becoming bigger, powerful, and her back straightens. Sue no longer feels vulnerable or scared, she is more frightened for the person who might attack her. Who would take on a silverback gorilla?

Find out who is your Animal Spirit and tune into their energy. Embrace their wonderful light into your life, and you will have some extraordinary moments.

A note from your Animal Spirit

I love you, even though my nature is kind, and gentle always remember:

When it comes to matters of protecting you,

I am powerful and relentless and will not let any harm come to you.

Just call my name, and I will be there for you.

Superhuman

You are superhuman, your thoughts and words are so powerful. If you continuously tell yourself that you are a failure, you cannot do it, and you are not good enough, etc. You will manifest a negative reality. Living in lower vibrations, you will attract many negative situations and create some awful problems for yourself. As mentioned in earlier chapters, this is not your fault, you have been conditioned and born into a negative world that wants you to live in this state. The people who run this world, I am not talking about the Prime Ministers or Presidents of the world, I am talking about the few elites who control our world, who are often known as The New World Order, Illuminati the Cabal, they are all the same thing: conditioning and controlling us to self-loathed and hate each other, causing a divide amongst us. They want us in this hazy and enslaved state to continue with our lives with our eyes shut; we are Shepard like sheep. They are keeping us in a lower vibration and controlling us by using fear and manipulation to feed their unhealthy appetite for greed. They do not want you to know how powerful you are. Did you know one of our superhuman strengths is that we have the power to self-heal? Many alternative holistic methods such as reflexology, acupuncture date back to Egyptian times or even further. Hieroglyphics showing a slave applying pressure points to someone's feet.

I also know from experience thoughts and words are extremely powerful.

True Story: Car Breakdown

It is rare if I ask for help, as I am the one everyone turns to. I do prefer it this way as it is my nature to help those in need. However, on this occasion, I needed help. It was a bit awkward for me to ask, but my car needed to go into the garage, and I needed a lift. I asked a friend and was shocked at her response. I have never seen her act this way, her ego god complex came out, and her words to me were shocking. I have known her for years, and whenever she needed help, I did not bat an eyelid, I was there for her, being kind and loving. Shocked by her god-like behaviour, I told her she could shove her help where the sun does not shine. I was angry and hurt, putting the phone down on her, my negatives thoughts escaped me. I wished her to be without her car for a week, as this would have a disastrous effect on her life, as she needed her car to earn money.

As soon as the thoughts went out, realising what I had done, I pleaded with the universe if I could take them back. It was just an instant moment that I had wished someone misfortune and instantly regretted it.

A day later, I received a phone call from my friend.

"Have you done something to my car?"

Instantly I thought she was suggesting that I had slashed or keyed her car.

"No!" I would not dream of causing any damage like that.

"What I mean, have you put a curse on my car? I know you were mad at me yesterday."

"I am so sorry, I did have a negative thought, but I tried to retract it."

"Max, you need to be careful!" she screamed down the phone at me.

"I'm sorry, I am still human. I couldn't help myself, what's the matter with your car?"

"The battery has gone on it, and the one I need is out of stock."

"Surely it's not? It's just a battery?"

"Phil (her husband) has been calling round to all the garages, the earliest I can get one is in a weeks' time."

I felt terrible for her, as they were both struggling financially, and this was a big blow for them, losing a week's money and paying out £120 for a battery.

Two weeks later, someone clipped my wing mirror, shattering the mirror. It would cost me almost £300, which I could not afford, so I asked for help from my Spiritual Family and told them that I was genuinely sorry for what I did to my friend, luckily it only ended up costing me £30 to repair.

So please be careful with your thoughts, especially if they are negative. Your thoughts and words are so powerful and used in this example, negative attracts negative. I wished my friend a misfortune, and in return, something unpleasant happened to my car.

There is a saying, what you put out into the universe, you will receive back. There have been countless times throughout my life where I have thought negatively about someone for it to come back with repercussions. So, imagine if you put out positive's thoughts, for example, sending out healing and loving thoughts to the people you know, wishing them good luck and abundance, look at all the goodness that will bounce back to you. You can take it a step further and wish love and healing thoughts to the planet and everything on it, this is something I do before going to sleep and thanking my beautiful Spiritual Family for their help, knowledge, and patients.

Your words and thoughts are your superhuman strength, try and be cheerful, with daily affirmations and positive thinking, you will manifest a higher vibration for yourself. The way to start addressing this is to start with yourself, show yourself some kindness, love, compassion, and healing.

Once you start your self-love journey, your vibration will increase, and the more you vibrate, the more positive things will come to you. Your bond with your Spiritual Family gets stronger, enabling you to open your mind to a new world of possibilities. This is an exciting journey, as you work with spirit in high-frequency, magical things will incur. You may find when healing someone, they might levitate of the bed, or find yourself levitating, you may be able to phase your hand through a solid object, being able to see other beings, having telepathic powers, etc. This may sound absurd to you, but we have been suppressed and conditioned, we only have access to ten per cent of our brains due to this. Imagine if you broke free from all your restraints and lived in higher frequency. What would be your superpower? The only way to start living in high frequency must come from within, you need to start loving yourself, and once you do, wow, what a beautiful and extraordinary world you would live in.

A note from Running Bear
When you believe, trust, and accept love for yourself, you will find the key to unlock your hidden powers. You will experience the most magical things in the world that will fill your heart with joy. You will understand there is more to this beautiful world than meets the eye. You are one of the awakening ones, shine your light so others can see their way out of the dark.

This is one of your superpowers.

Nature

When you are in a dark place, self-loathing taking over your life, you feel drained, tired, everything is such an effort. In this dismal emotional state, most people retreat, some consume multitudes of alcohol, some may take drugs or do both to shut things out. I found drinking alcohol in this state was highly destructive for me. Consuming high quantities led to my attempt to end my life, thankfully, my Angel intervened and saved my life. Alcohol and drugs are natural depressants and will enhance self-loathing.

After my second divorce and losing my family home, I found a house for my children. With all the turmoil and trauma, I had experienced, hating that I was still alive, I retreated to my bedroom, which I painted the walls black. I would sit for hours in the dark day after day, hating my life, hating people who had hurt me, but most of all, hating myself.

I even spent that Christmas in my room, which was not like me.

Friends and family would visit me daily, sitting on my bed telling me their woes and problems. I would listen even though my head was screaming, leave me alone, I cannot handle this right now. I was a mother, a good friend, a loving daughter, I would try and help whenever possible, but I could not wait for them to leave me alone.

True Story: Little Birds
One sunny afternoon sitting on my bed, there was a small gap

between my curtains, the sun shone brightly into my room. For some reason, I was drawn to my window, drawing the curtains back. I was bedazzled by several little sparrows, all taking turns to bath in a small puddle on my drive. I stood there, watching them for several minutes. I felt the corners of my mouth turning up, joy filling my heart.

The next day the sun shone again, even though it was slightly raining. I rushed to the window, to my surprise there was a beautiful rainbow, the little birds were bathing in the puddle again, there were two squirrels on my front lawn scurrying around on the ground. I felt the dark cloud above me lifting and happiness, filling my whole being. Watching nature was the start of me climbing out of my pit.

The beautiful rainbow, the trees that swayed to the rhythm of the wind, the little sparrows chirping, and taking their daily bath, the squirrels hopping around, the warmth of the sun, made me want to sit outside.

Sitting there in my garden, I watched the bumblebees hovering over the lavender, the white butterflies dancing around. I had a beautiful green dragonfly who would visit me frequently. I would listen to the blackbirds singing their sweet melodies.

From my garden, I started to venture to my local beach, sitting on the pebbly shore. I would inhale the salty air, closing my eyes, I would listen to the flow of the waves, I would take a deep breathe in and when I exhaled, I felt my troubles, stresses and worries were washed away.

I was living in the now, no longer trapped in the past. I let go of all my fears for my future. I felt peace, stillness, and happiness.

Nature is beautiful, it is such a powerful healing place. If you are stuck in a rut, things getting onto top of you, whether you live in a flat, house, caravan, just pop your head out. You will find something amazing.

I do not like spiders, especially if they are on me, but I would never kill one. One frosty morning, sitting in my little garden, I saw a beautiful spider's web, sparkling and glistening. The intricate pattern this tiny spider had woven was remarkable.

The tiniest things when we start to notice brings us joy and being in nature brings us back to Now, the Present, giving us clarity to cleanse our minds. I find these situations are where my epiphany appears, giving me great understanding and upliftment.

Start today, even if you have a hectic life.

Spare five minutes out in the air and watch nature, whether it is raining, snowing, or windy, stand at your window, sit in your car. Watch the rain dance upon the pavement. Watch the lighting light up the dark sky. My favourite is sunsets when the sky is full of pretty colours of pinks, oranges, and purples. At night I love looking up at the moon, especially when it is full. Mother nature is truly remarkable.

Running Bear says, try a meditation in nature. It is truly a magnificent way to connect to the spirit world. What is your guide saying to you? What does your loved ones advise you to do? Listen to your Angel and your Spirit Animal. Connect with your higher self. The first thing that pops into your mind is them, listening to what they are saying to you. Do not be afraid to answer them back. I bet they are telling you that you are loved, and you are truly special.

Fairies and other Magical Beings

Fairies and other magical beings are real, I have been fortunate enough to have seen them myself.

There are different types of fairies, but the ones that frequent me most are the little brown woodlands fairies. What is their purpose? Why do I see them? Why do they visit me? I have asked these questions over the years. It was not until I started my self-love journey that I started to find out the answers.

True Story: Superman

One sunny afternoon, I had some bad news. I felt a big dark cloud looming over me. I was struggling with the horrible thoughts that flooded my mind. I so wanted to pick up my ugly stick and torture myself while another part of me was shouting out, "be kind to yourself." I was in a whirlwind of mixed emotions until…

I was standing in my living room when a beautiful brown fairy about four inches long flew across my room.

Usually, they are so quick, but this one flew in slow motion, I could see his smiling porcelain face beaming at me.

He had one arm stretched out in front of him, imitating Superman.

I laughed and laughed. Yes, I am a geek, I love DC and Marvel, and to see this little being doing the Superman pose extinguished the dark cloud above my head. I felt my whole person coming back to life, the horrible thoughts disappeared, and NO! I did not want to pick up my ugly stick. I brought myself back to the here and now, and I was super thrilled that this little fairy had brought me so much joy.

On your self-love journey, you will be faced with many challenges, and there will be times when you feel sad, which is okay, we are allowed to have these days so we can appreciate the good ones, but it is not okay to beat yourself up.

The fairies are drawn to people who are on their self-love journey as you are evolving into your true self. You become a better version of yourself, caring for yourself and others, but you are considerate and compassionate about your environment, nature, and the world.

These little fairies that visit me come at a time when I need upliftment and encouragement. Once you are on your self-love journey, do not be surprised when they come to visit you.

True Story: Celestial Fairies

A good friend of mine who suffers terribly with her health has type one diabetes, and unfortunately, she has had many life-threatening lows. Emma had a terrible feeling that she was not long for this world, she feared she did not have much of a future and formed a negative magnet. It took time for her to accept love for herself, but something incredible happened when she began. Most nights, she had tiny little white fairies coming to visit her.

Lying in bed, Emma would stretch out her arm where these little celestial fairies would hop onto her arm. They gave her healing, hope, and helped her to believe in herself. Emma never thought she would have a future because of her illness, now she is a fantastic medium helping others, and her fairies frequently visit her.

True Story: My Dragons

When I came into full force to work for spirit, I came under attack by the dark side. At this time, my celestial dragons appeared, and to this day they surround me with their love and protection.

One night returning home from seeing a client, it was dark and eerie driving on the motorway. It was 11.45 p.m. and there was not a car or lorry insight. Driving home, a felt a sense of heavy dread, the sky around me seemed to get darker and darker. My spidery senses were off the scale, warning me of danger. There was so much turbulence around my car, I felt I was driving in a tornado, my car battling against the wind, holding tight onto my steering wheel to keep my car straight. Winding down my window, there was no breeze, just silence. Looking down at my speed monitor, I thought I was driving at 70mph, but my car struggled to do 40mph. Suddenly, the sky lit up in a magnificent red, then something weighty landed on the roof of my car. I jumped out of my skin. Another flash of red light but this time, I saw a giant dragon flying beside me and another above me protecting me. I felt like I was in the scene of Jurassic Park when the man is racing through the forest on a motorbike with his raptors running alongside him. The twenty minute journey home seemed endless, the sky lighting up around me and more debris hitting my car. Getting home, I raced indoors terrified but so grateful for my dragons keeping me safe. The next morning, I was dreading going out to see the state of my car. I knew with all the debris hitting it, that for sure it would be severely damaged. I was shocked and surprised while inspecting my vehicle, there was no damage at all.

You are probably wondering what was attacking me? There is evil in this world, and Running Bear told me there are such things as demons. A small group of them wanted to recruit me for the dark side, if they were not successful, they were to destroy me. I was baffled why they went for little old me? Running Bear told me that I was going to help a lot of people. My jaw dropped; I have heard this before when I saw the Angel.

These lower level beings tried their best to terrify me for a short period, but my dragons never left my side.

True Story: Bob
Many other magical beings are all helping and guiding us. I would like to introduce you to my little blue alien that I have called Bob. Yes, a blue alien. He is the size of a nine year-old boy and is the typical egg-shaped head of an alien with a skinny body. He appeared to me about two years ago. I first saw him standing in the doorway of my kitchen door, then another time he was sat on my kitchen side. I told my family and friends about him, which they thought I had really lost the plot. I would often speak to him, and I know intuitively he was here to help me.

One evening, I was telling my son about Bob.

At the time, my son was only twenty-three years old, he was standing in the kitchen doorway.

My son has a great sense of humour and was teasing me about how crazy I sounded. We were both giggling as he told me he needed to call the men in the white coats to come and take me away.

Suddenly there was a loud bang in the kitchen, my son went white and froze to the spot.

"What was that?" He looked shocked.

"That's Bob," I giggled.

"No! Mum, what was that?"

"Have a look."

He turned around and popped on the kitchen light.

"Mum," he yelled. "Look!"

All the kitchen cupboards and drawers were all open. The contents underneath the sink were all placed neatly on the floor. What was more shocking, Jack was the last person in the kitchen as he was the one blocking the doorway.

"That's Bob, he's playing a trick on you," I joked.

"I'm getting out of here." He looked bewildered and frightened.

One morning I received a phone from an old friend I had not seen for a while, she was a lovely medium who needed my help. I popped round to her house and had a cuppa with her. Early that morning, I saw Bob standing at my bedroom door as I awoke. She asked me what had been going on in my life, I was bursting at the seams to tell her about my little alien friend, who I had randomly called Bob. Instead of judging me or thinking I was bonkers, Jane asked inquisitively what he looked like. I described him to her, but to my amazement, she stood up from the table and told me to follow her. We went into the living room, where she pulled open a draw on her dressers, she turned around with a drawing in her hand.

I gasped as she said, "Is this, Bob?"

It was a beautiful drawing of Bob, my little blue alien friend.

"That's Bob!" I was shocked.

Jane told me her friend, who is a psychic artist, had drawn this for her about a year or so ago, she too had a little blue alien friend, but she called him something different.

They are here to help us and our planet.

You can imagine I was thrilled it was not just only me, there are many of them out there helping us, you never know you might have one helping you, keep a lookout.

True Story: The Wind

I was about nine years old. One bright early morning, I was

suddenly awoken by the growling noise of the wind. It sounded so violent and fierce. I could hear something being tossed and smashed around the back garden.

Feeling afraid, I was curious enough to peep through my curtains. I was shocked and mortified at what I saw. I held my breath as, remaining still as a statue, I watched the monster picking up my brother's go-kart and smashing it around the garden. The beast stood like a man covered from head to toe in fur, it looked angry as it bared its big fangs. I had never seen anything like it. I was petrified. Slowly retreating to my warm, safe bed, I remained quiet and still, waiting patiently for Dad to get up. I could still hear the growling and smashing noises as I placed my trembling hands over my ears – it seemed forever till Dad got up.

Hearing my parents getting up, I bolted from my room, catching Dad on the landing while Mum went downstairs.

"Dad! Dad!" I panicked.

Dad turned towards me.

"Dad, there's a thing, a thing in the garden… it's smashing up Lee's go-kart!" I cried.

Dad was startled by how terrified I looked.

"It's OK, I will have a look!" he tried to reassure me.

"What's happen to my go-kart?" Lee opened his door. He was still half asleep.

Ignoring him, I followed Dad to the kitchen where Mum was putting the kettle on. I watched Dad go over to the back door and unlock it; I shuddered in fright.

Watching Dad go out of the back door, I prayed that thing was not still there.

"Pearl! Come here!" I heard Dad shout from the garden.

I watched Mum vanish through the back door. Feeling

156

nervous, I started to bite my bottom lip.

"What's going on?"

I almost jumped out of my skin as my brother stood behind me. I was too speechless to answer him. Suddenly Dad reappeared with Mum.

"What did you see?" Dad asked with a severe look in his eyes.

"I saw, I saw a monster, it looked like a cross between a Werewolf and Big Foot; it was smashing up Lee's go-kart!" I blurted out.

"My go-kart?" Lee raced past both my parents and me into the garden; I could hear him screaming.

I stood and stared at Dad.

"The go-kart has been smashed to pieces, it's all around the garden!"

I felt my heart was about to explode from my chest, I was so scared and terrified.

"It must have been the wind that did it," Mum intervened.

I wished she were right, but both Dad and I knew that was not true.

Thirty years later, one night, Elisha, my daughter aged nineteen years, came bursting through the front door. I was startled as she exploded into the living room.

"MUM! MUM! You're not going to believe it!" She seemed over-excited.

"What?" I was curious.

"You know your Wind Story?"

"Yeah." A cold shiver ran up my spine.

"Someone else saw it too!"

Elisha told me that she had met some of his best mates when

she was out with her boyfriend. She had always kept quiet about our spiritual experiences, not everyone believes. Being in a new relationship, she wanted to make a good impression, so she never mentioned her spooky stories to him.

There was a large group of them all congregated around a table inside the pub. Taking a seat, Simon, her boyfriend, introduced her to his friends. Elisha being shy amongst new people, remained quiet. As she sat and listened to his friends, they all got onto the subject of what was the scariest moment of your life. They all took it in turns to tell their stories. One boy started to tell his story, and Elisha's jaw dropped.

When he was a young boy around nine years old, he could hear the wind growling and something smashing one early morning as he lay in bed. Peeping through his curtains, he saw this thing – a beast! It looked like a man with arms and legs, but it was not a man, it was tall and covered in thick matted hair with big snarling fangs. It was smashing up the patio set. He said it was the scariest moment in his life.

For years when I heard the wind howling, it would take me back in time to that harrowing morning, but working with Running Bear, I no longer feared the wind. He told me other beings are living amongst us, even though this beast looked terrifying to me, Running Bear told me he was a gentle creature that would not harm us. He followed on to say these creatures were angry, if you notice, these beings were attacking the Go-Kart and patio set, which were all made from plastic. They knew plastic would cause significant harm to our planet. When I saw this being, it was the 1970's and then sighted again in 2000. Now in the present day, plastic is such a vast concern causing damaging effects globally.

The age is quite relevant as younger children can see more than adults as they are new to this world. Have you seen anything like this? If so, do not be scared, Hollywood has a lot to answer for. They know there are other beings in this world living beside us, so they have made horror films to scare us. These beautiful beings may look like us, or some may be disguised, or you may have the privilege to see them in their natural form. Their purpose is to help us and our planet.

A note from your magical beings

We are standing beside you, always showing signs that we are here to help you.

Start to believe in us, and this will open a world of magic that we can freely communicate.

Speak to us about your dreams and passions, and we will assist in providing high vibrational frequency to help you manifest your desires.

All you need to do is unlock your mind, allowing new possibilities to come your way. Throw doubt and fear into the wind. Remember, you are a powerful being, and anything is possible.

Just believe.

Animal Magic

You are probably wondering why animals have anything to do with self-love. Animals are magical creatures, their energy uplifting and wonderous. Animals can allow us to share extraordinary moments with them. When they do, no matter how low you feel, these beautiful creatures can instantly transform your whole being from negative to positive.

True story: Furry Friends
I had an appointment at the hospital. I had to have my heart scanned and speak to my consultant, about whether my arteries were furring up. As you can imagine, I was petrified and worried about my future.

My mother lived close to the hospital, hospital parking was a nightmare, so I parked at ums. On the way back home, the results were positive, I felt relieved, but I was also feeling a bag of mixed emotions. With all the worrying and stress leading up to the appointment, it had taken its toll on me. With my head all over the place, walking back to mums, to my left-hand side was a 4ft iron fence that surrounded the large courtyard that led to my mother's home.

Heading towards the gate, which was about 100 metres away, I notice something furry in the small bushes on the other side of the fence. Literally, it was by my ankles. "Good morning, Mr Squirrel. How are you today?" No, I am not Mrs Doctor Dolittle. This little creature had such a cute little face, I could see him smiling at me. As I continued to walk, this little squirrel walked close by my side while I was having a little chat with him. As I reach the gate, I expected him to scurry off, but he waited for me to enter and continued to walk with me up the pathway. My little companion walked me to my mother's door. I was amazed and fascinated by him.

As soon as I thanked him for this special moment, he scurried off. I went into my mums filled with delight and happiness, she wanted to hear how I got on at the hospital, but I could not help telling her about my little friend who had walked me home.

I could write countless stories about these special moments I have had with deer, badgers, foxes, tigers, elephants, dogs, birds, and my special little cat. They all had one thing in common, these special moments all came when I was feeling low. It is natural for us to have bad moments; it makes us appreciate the good times. All I am asking is to take note, I reckon your dog, cat, whatever furry nonfurry being you have, instinctively knows when you are feeling sad. Look closely into their eyes, and you will see how much they love you.

True Story: The Deer
Even if you do not have a furry companion or may be allergic to them, you just go outside when you are feeling low. After my stepfather lost his Golden Retriever Jeb, he was beside himself.

One morning he took himself up to the woods that Jeb loved. There was a massive log on the ground, and my stepfather sat upon it. His face in his hands, as tears strolled down his face, how he missed his loving dog. Suddenly, he felt something on his shoulder, he lowered his hands and turned his head to see a beautiful deer resting her chin upon his shoulder. He could not believe his eyes, he sat quietly with her for a few moments till she left. He came home beaming with joy, telling us what had just happened.

Animals love us unconditionally, they do not judge, discriminate, or abuse us, their love heals us.

A note from Running Bear

Animals are healing, having a cat on your lap purring is healthier than any prescription in the world, as the vibrations you are receiving are of the most genuine love and happiness.

Pay attention and feel the remarkable healing your furry love one is giving you.

You are loved and adored.

Food

Food? What does food have to do with loving ourselves? Food plays a vital role, eating the wrong kind of food can poison our body, encouraging the whole central system to become toxic, which can develop into life-threatening diseases such as cancer, diabetes, heart problems, etc., whereas eating the right kind of foods can balance our bodies and enhanced the self-healing process. In essence, the food we eat can harm or heal us.

When I was depressed for several years, my diet was shocking, I could not cook for myself, was not motivated, no energy, or the will to cook myself a healthy meal. It was easier to order takeaways and munch on lots of chocolate and crisps. I put on a lot of weight, which made me even more depressed, and I ended up being diagnosed with diabetes type two.

When you have depression, you can go one of two ways, one is to comfort eat, whereas some people stop eating for days, but now and then they will gorge themselves on eating the wrong kind of food. Starving themselves, they may be losing weight, but they are causing such stress and harm on their vital organs, which can cause health complications, and further down the line, they end up with an eating disorder.

Eating the right kind of foods will raise your vibration, improve the way you feel about yourself, and your lifestyle. Working with Running Bear and my Spiritual Family on my self-love journey, my eating habit has changed naturally. All my life, I loved my chocolate, there was not a day that would not go by without me having my chocolate. I never once said to myself I should give it up, but once I started my self-love journey, I naturally stop eating it. It began with the taste, I no longer liked it, and I no longer enjoyed it. At the same time, I fancied a glass of wine every now and then, but even that, I no longer relished. Eating meat was becoming an issue, I could not eat the bacon sandwiches that I used to love, it tasted of death and despair in my mouth. I asked my Spiritual Family, are you turning me vegetarian? They showed me eating chocolate, drinking alcohol, and eating meat were lowering my vibrations.

To be truly one with yourself, you need to eat high vibrational food.

It does not matter where you are on the spectrum, whether you like your drink, eat chocolate or meat, or you may be already a vegetarian or vegan. When you start to love yourself, you will go through a natural process of eating the high vibrational foods that make you feel alive.

If you can, eat coconut in its raw form as it is the highest vibrational food, it is known as a superfood. Eating pieces of coconut daily helps heal all the chakras. Eating anything raw like vegetables and fruit are all high in vibration. Cooking your vegetables does decrease the high vibrational frequency, but they are still considered high vibration.

Blending your vegetables or fruit into a juice is fantastic for you. When eating, it takes your body a lot of energy to digest your food, having blended your food will give your digestive system a small break, which means it has more power to concentrate on the self-healing process.

Try and have one blended juice a day with high vibrational foods, do not forget to try and get organic food as this is the best, but do not worry if you cannot, it is still good for you. I have a

164

lovely, blended juice for my breakfast.

See if you can make a blended juice for each chakra's colour, as this will heal your chakra you are working on. You can make a little diary in your journal:

Monday – red juice for my root, breakfast.

Tuesday – orange juice for my sacral, mid-afternoon etc.

Drinking caffeine such as coffee, tea, and energy drinks are also low vibrational, again, I liked my coffees and teas, but once I started my self-love journey, I naturally gravitated to water.

Start being aware, take notes down in your journal. When we began this beautiful journey, we will not just gravitate to positive people and situations, we are forever evolving, and our Spiritual Family will naturally help you make better decisions for yourself. Instead of reaching out for a bar of chocolate, you may find that you end up eating a carrot!

Journal

I have mentioned writing your dreams, messages from spirit, writing down your mediations, etc. into a journal. It is essential to record your experiences. As mentioned before, you may not understand it now, but your future self may have a realisation that could help you understand your situation, purpose, and path. Another reason to keep a journal, especially doing the self-love exercises, after a few months, you will feel so differently about yourself. You will see your growth, which will enable you to reflect and become more aware of yourself and everyone around you. Another vital tool for keeping up your journey is to write down your thoughts. If you have a bad day, write down all the details and everything that you feel, even when you are harsh on yourself. We can have bad days that make us sad, we need negatives to appreciate beauty and light. The following day or when you are feeling better, write yourself a little note under all the bad things you have written about yourself in your journal. Step out of yourself for a moment, what would you write to a dear friend if they felt that low about themselves?

Write some kind words and forgive yourself.

Exercise 13 "Why do I Hate myself?"
In your journal, write down, why do you hate yourself?

Look a little bit deeper, where did it come from? Has someone said this to you? If so, would you consider them a nice person? When they said it, were they angry? What is their background? What are their fears? Keep asking yourself more questions.

For example

I hate myself because I am fat.

Where did it come from?

I have just had a baby.

I feel insecure about my weight and body.

My husband keeps on about my weight.

My husband says horrible things to me, I consider him to be mean.

My husband was not angry when he says it, he likes to say it to me as he knows it upsets me.

He has loving parents, but he is the only child. He likes to get his own way, and he tends to be selfish. He is afraid of being alone.

Once you have written it down, get a dearly trusted friend to look at your list. Having a different perspective can shed new light on the matter, which can give you a significant epiphany.

Write underneath your list your findings.

Example: I have discovered that I am not fat, I am beautiful and proud to be me, my husband is so scared of losing me that he is going to the extreme extent to make me feel like rubbish, to make him feel better. I do not deserve to be treated this way. I ask for healing for him and myself.

Keep documenting your feelings, insecurities, and fears. Open your mind and question every aspect of their origins. Where did this come from? Why did this happen? Etc.

Take note each time you felt low, what happened around you. Reading this book has started or advancing your awakening, you are now more susceptible of feeling, hearing, and seeing the beautiful magic all around us. Take note each time you felt low, what happened around you. I bet something amazing happened, just lift up your chin and you will be able to see.

True Story: Rapist

A man in my local area had been targeting young girls aged between fourteen – sixteen years old, he prowled the streets late at night to find his victim so he could brutally rape her. The police made an appeal on TV expressing their concerns, they stated with each victim he was becoming more violent. They feared he would kill the next girl. Their advice was for young teenage girls not to go out in the evening.

At the time it was Paige's eleventh birthday which meant I was only in my early thirties. One sunny August afternoon I parked in an open car park in the town centre. Once I finished shopping, for Paige's birthday presents, I returned to my car carrying bags of goodies. Putting the bags on the back seat I quickly hopped into the car and put the key into the ignition. The car was scorching hot, the air was stifling. As I put my finger onto the electric button to open my window, I suddenly heard a man from behind me shouting.

"DON'T!"

Startled and frightened, I thought someone was in my car. I slowly turned round with my heart pounding heavily in my chest, I was relieved and shocked to find no one was there.

"LOCK THE DOORS!"

I jumped out of my skin. Who was it? Where was it coming from? I started to panic and hit the button locking all the doors. I was gasping for air as the heat was suffocating me, but I was too afraid to open my window. I put on the air conditioning and as the cool breeze blew over me, I took in a deep breath. I could feel my heart slowing down.

Suddenly there was a tap on my window, I felt my heart jump up into my mouth. A young man in his late twenties with short blonde hair and a thick blonde moustache stood smiling at me. He looked friendly; I was about to undo the window.

"DON'T! GO NOW! GET OUT OF HERE!"

I felt my heart racing again as panic set in, shaking and trembling, I quickly glanced around the car park, there was no one around except for this man and me.

"Excuse me, is this is a Renault Espace?" enquired the man. Not wanting to be rude.

"Yes, it is!" I replied nervously.

"DON'T SPEAK TO HIM! GO NOW!"

I felt my whole-body trembling in fear. What was happening? Why was I so scared?

"My wife wants one of these, is there any chance you would be able to let me in and let me have a look round?" He smiled.

"NO!"

Feeling jittery and nervous I turned the key.

"I'm sorry but I'm late… I have to pick up my daughter," I lied.

"It will only take a minute of your time,' he pleaded.

"GO NOW! NOW!"

"Sorry I can't."

With my heart beating so fast I knew I had to get away. I wheel-spun out of the car park. I raced off down the road doing more than the speed limit. I was in such a hurry to get home. Trembling and shaking in fear, tears were welling up into my eyes. I was relieved when I saw my husband's car parked outside our house.

I burst in through the front door and my husband was standing in the hallway.

"Oh my god! What's the matter with you?" He looked startled.

The last time he saw me in such a state was when I called his uncle a nonce.

"Do I want to hear this?" His face tightened.

I could hardly stand. Collapsing onto the floor, I gazed up at him and told him what happened. I could not believe his reaction, he looked down at me laughing hysterically. He told me I was being stupid and silly. I argued back telling him I should tell the police. He laughed at me even more, telling me he had never heard anything so ridiculous. I felt exhausted and inflated as he convinced me that it was all in my mind.

Three weeks later, as I was sitting watching the evening news with my husband, my jaw dropped as the presenter announced the police had caught the rapist. They displayed a picture of a man in his late twenties with short blonde hair and a thick blonde moustache.

"It was him!" I gasped.

"What?" My husband was annoyed I had interrupted him.

"That is the man who came up to me in the car park, it was him!"

I now know the man shouting at me in the car was my beautiful guide Running Bear, and I am so glad that I listen to him but reflecting upon this story it was obvious that I had low self-esteem, no self-worth as I allowed my husband to belittle and talk down to me. He had convinced me that I was overreacting and being silly. Today, I am a completely different person. I believe that I am a better version of my true self and as time goes by and continuing to love myself, I am evolving.

I had written this story down in my journal about twenty years ago, even though it was a shocking story but a beautiful example how my guide helped me, it also showed me I was in an abusive relationship. Therefore, writing in your journal no matter how many experiences you have, writing your story is your proof of how far you have come, it does not have to be twenty years which seems to be a different lifetime to me, it could be one year, three months or weeks to see your growth. This will give you your spark that will enable you to continue you on your self-love journey. Keep up the good work, keep writing your experience, keep asking those questions and you will be rewarded with so much abundance, joy, laughter, and peace. Your life will remarkably change for the better.

Going through my journals I found this lovely story that happened to me about fifteen years ago, it brings me so much joy and laughter that I thought that I would share this with you.

True Story: Practical Joke
Before going to bed I stood on the landing and whispered to my children…

"Goodnight Paige!"

"Goodnight Elisha!"

No reply, how strange? They must have been tired and fallen fast asleep as soon as their heads hit the pillow. Going into my room, taking all my clothes off, and putting on my nightie, I could not wait to jump into bed. I switched off my light and pulled back my duvet. I was just about to leap into bed when suddenly, to my shock and horror, something from underneath my bed grabbed both of my ankles. I screamed and screamed as I jumped in terror. I quickly smacked on my light, my heart was almost pounding out of my chest and, breathing heavily, I could hear laughter. I tried to take deep breaths to calm myself down as my eyes were drawn to the two laughing heads that appeared from underneath my bed. I felt instant relief and a flush of anger at seeing Paige and Elisha laughing hysterically underneath my bed.

Through their hysteria they found it difficult to climb out from underneath the bed. I was not amused and refused to help them, eventually the mischievous pair managed to clamber out.

"You little *******!" I cursed them.

"You frightened the life out of me!" I yelled at both, placing my hand on my poor heart.

The pair could not contain themselves and they went off to bed in fits of laughter.

The next night when I shouted out goodnight, I made sure I got a reply from each of them. There was no way I wanted a repeat of the night before. Hearing them replying I knew they were in their own bedrooms; I was safe to go to bed. I got undressed and put my nightie on, then jumped into bed and let out a relaxing sigh. It was a warm night, I was already getting hot so, kicking the duvet off my legs, I felt myself instantly cooling down. Closing my eyes, I started to slowly drift off when suddenly someone grabbed both of my ankles. I let out a piecing scream as my heart pounded so hard in my chest, for a split second I thought it was going to burst out.

"You little *******!" I screamed.

Bolting up in bed and retracting my legs close to me, I waited for the laughter. Staring hard at the silent darkness at the end of my bed I waited for the girls to appear.

"Mum, you, OK?" gasped Paige as I heard her racing to my bedroom door.

"Mum! Mum! What's wrong?" shouted Elisha who was closely behind Paige.

"Can you please pop the light on?" I said, again placing my hand on my heart.

"What happened?" asked Paige as she put on the light, came in the bedroom, and took a seat next to me.

"You two…did you creep in and grabbed my ankles?"

Staring at the end of the bed I knew the answer before asking the question.

"NO!" both said simultaneously, they both looked terrified.

I check all around my bedroom room, including underneath my bed and in the wardrobes, it was evident there was no one else in the room with me.

After a couple of hours, I bravely went back to bed, making sure my legs were not exposed. I said a little prayer and asked whoever did it not to do it again. Since then, touch wood, there have been no more practical jokes from spirit. Wish I could say the same about the children!

In this instant I knew who the mischief maker was, my grandad in spirit loved to play practical jokes on me when he was here on the earth plane, and since then he has behaved.

Having uplifting stories to show us that we are truly not on our own, whether they are playing tricks on you, moving objects, or giving you signs is wonderful to know that there is more to life than just us.

True Story: Hi Dad

One summer evening, I was coming home from visiting a friend. I pulled up and parked my WRX outside my house. I got out of the car and walked towards my front porch.

"Oh no," I thought aloud.

"I've left my mobile phone in the car!"

I turned around and went to unlock my car.

I just screamed! I could not believe my eyes! My dad was sat in the driver's seat with his Elvis Presley sunglasses on. He had a big grin on his face, and he held up his hand with his fist clenched and thumb sticking up. I could see him as clearly as when he was alive. With all the commotion, my children came running out of the house. I turned round to face them all and told them what I had seen. I glanced back over my shoulder; my dad had now vanished.

I was feeling shocked and bewildered.

I knew there was a reason he was here.

This obviously meant something!

At that time, my boyfriend had been continuously nagging at me to get rid of my car. Later, I found out that he was extremely jealous that I had one of the fastest cars on the road and that my car was better than his! Anyway, with his constant nagging, I was getting to a point where he had almost convinced me that I should get rid of my Scooby.

Thanks to my dad's appearance, I did not get rid of my car in the end. Instead, I got rid of the boyfriend!

I found this little experience in my journal. During that time, I endure a lot of mental abuse from my boyfriend for a considerable time. With his abuse, it was wearing me out, and I almost surrendered to his needs. My dad showed up in the nick of time to give me the strength and courage to end things. Looking back on this experience, I will never let anyone abuse me in such away.

True Story: Warning
I wrote down this nightmare that I kept having in my journal.

It was a bright sunny morning. The children and I were all in the car heading towards a new swimming complex.

We were all excited; we were so looking forward to the

flume rides and leisurely floating around the park on a giant rubber ring. Looking at the brochure at the Haven site where we were all staying, it looked amazing.

We arrived at the destination, and I parked in their car park when suddenly I was overwhelmed by a horrible sensation. Glancing up at the magnificent shiny new building, my stomach knotted. 'Don't go in there!' The voice in my head screamed, who I now know was Running Bear.

Trying to shake off this feeling, we all got out of the car and headed for the building. As we entered the place, I tried so hard to ignore the frantic warning in my head.

"Mum, look, there's the flume rides!" Pointed Paige excitedly.

"Mum, can me and Brooke go swimming?" Elisha had spotted the big pool with a water fountain in it.

"Mum, can me and Jack go over there?" Brodie pointed to the ring ride.

What was going on? Why was I so worried? All my children are good swimmers. Looking around the complex, there were lifeguards everywhere. Where was the danger? I watched my children scatter in different directions, but I could not help but keep my eyes on Brodie and Jack. Was it because they were the younger ones? I was not sure. I had a horrible feeling that I thought something terrible was going to happen.

I watched the lifeguard safely placing Brodie and Jack onto their rubber rings. It was a small narrow stream that gently flowed around the park, the water was extremely shallow. Why was I paranoid?

Suddenly I heard a big gush of water; I could not believe my eyes. It was like a huge tidal wave sprouting out of the stream just in front of Brodie and Jack; suddenly, a giant killer whale appeared and took both of my children into its mouth, swallowing them whole. I screamed and screamed.

Bolting up in bed and realising it was only a nightmare, I felt relief filling my heart. For the last week, I kept having the same nightmare. It was rare to have the same repeated nightmare.

The last continuous nightmare was when I kept dreaming about the lions; now, looking back, I could understand why, but why was I experiencing these nightmares? I was not in a relationship, I had no one abusing or controlling me.

I was at university; the course was going well; I was managing okay financially. In a few months, I had planned to take the kids on holiday, so why was I getting these horrific images?

Four months later, forgetting about the nightmare, I took the children to a Haven site for a short holiday break, staying in one of their luxurious caravans. Looking around the place to find out what activities they had, I came across a brochure.

The site was not so far from a new swimming complex with various flumes rides and other water activities. The children eagerly looked through the brochure; they all thought it would be amazing. At the front of the pamphlet was a shiny new building that housed all these fantastic rides. Something about it seemed familiar.

"I've been here!" I mumbled to myself.

"When?" Elisha promptly answered me.

"I'm not sure, but I swear I have been here!"

"Mum, you're going mad, it's not long been open!" Paige pointed to the text which displayed the date.

"Yeah, you're right!" I tried shaking it off.

One bright sunny morning, packing up our bathers and towels, we all headed for the swimming park. The children were so excited and looking forward to the flumes and other water rides. Pulling up in the car park and looking for a place to park, I caught a glimpse of the shiny new building in front of me. I stopped the car in its tracks, my stomach knotted, I felt sick.

"I've been here before!" I shouted.

"Mum, you can't stop here!" scolded Brooke as she looked over her shoulder to find the car behind us having to perform an emergency stop.

Ignoring all the commotion around me, I suddenly remembered the nightmare and losing Brodie and Jack; the very thought tore a big hole in my heart.

"Mum, move the car!"

Coming to, I was trembling. I quickly parked in space, but I had to tell them before they could all jump out.

"Look, we can't go in there!"

"What? Why not?" asked Paige.

"Look! I've got a horrible feeling; I've dreamt of this place… something bad is going to happen!"

"Mum! Don't be silly… don't worry," Elisha tried to reassure me.

"What bad things?" Brodie was curious.

"I dreamt that you and Jack were eaten by a killer whale in there!" I was still trembling.

"That's nice… thanks a lot!" Brodie replied while the other children laughed.

"I'm serious… I know something is going to happen!"

"Mum, don't worry, it was just a dream, I promise you there are not going to be any killer whales in there," Paige said in a patronizing tone.

"I know that I know it sounds daft to you lot, but…"

Finally, I gave in; maybe I was silly and overprotective, but

177

I still could not shake off this horrible feeling.

Gingerly walking into the complex, I was shocked and amazed to find a swimming pool with a water fountain. Elisha and Brooke ran off together, both simultaneously jumping into the pool. I felt my stomach twist; I felt sick when I saw the rubber ring ride that slowly drifted you around the park.

"Don't go! That is where you die," I found myself saying out loud to Brodie and Jack.

They both glanced over their shoulders and laughed.

"Don't worry, Mum! I will watch out for Willy!" joked Jack.

"Mum, you're terrible, come on… the flumes are over there." Brooke placed her hand into mine. Glancing around the complex, there were lifeguards everywhere.

Was I being silly?

Suddenly Paige appeared, dripping wet.

"Mum, I will go with Brodie and Jack!" She could see that I was worried sick.

Knowing their older sister was with them gave me peace of mind. I watched Paige chase after them. I turned around, and Elisha was standing dripping wet behind me.

"Flume rides!" She beamed a smile at me.

Feeling a bit better, I darted off with my two girls heading for the flumes. While queuing, Elisha decided that she would go down the flume first, followed by Brooke, then me. I was happy with that order.

Coming down the wet slippery flume, which was so much fun, the big smile on my face soon vanished. Waiting at the end of the flume were Paige, Brodie, and Elisha; they looked distraught. Quickly jumping to my feet, I felt my heart stop. I quickly scanned the place. Where was Brodie? Where was Jack? I glanced back at the girls.

"Mum… Mum… they're OK… they're in the changing rooms getting dressed!" Suddenly, Paige burst into tears.

I threw my arms around her.

"What happened?" I asked calmly, even though I was climbing the walls in sheer panic.

"They almost drowned… the lifeguards are stupid… if I hadn't been there, they would have died!" she sobbed.

I darted off to the changing room; my two babies looked stressed and traumatized. Paige went on to explain what had happened.

The popular floating ring ride had a steep slide that catapults you off the ring into a small 6ft pool. This section was surrounded by lifeguards who were too busy talking to each other and being complete idiots. Only one person should go down the slide at a time. Jack went down the slide, followed by Brodie, and another five children came down the slide simultaneously and landed on top of them. Sheer panic set in as the five children could not swim; being out of their depth, they crushed Brodie and Jack further and further towards the bottom of the pool. They tried to fight their way to the surface, only to be pushed back under. Luckily, Paige was next down the slide, and she saw what was happening. Being a lot bigger and stronger than the other kids, she dived to the bottom of the pool and rescued her brother and sister, putting them on the side. Both Brodie and Jack were crying between coughing and spluttering. Paige lifted herself out of the pool while all the lifeguards just stood and stared.

After hearing what happened, everything clicked into place. The nightmares had been a warning.

"Right, let's get out of this place!"

There were no arguments; we all got dressed and headed back to the park.

Ask for Protection

Your Spiritual Family, who lovingly surrounds you, wants to protect all of you, including your auric field.

But they need your permission, except Angels. Who has friends or family members, after spending some time in their company, has felt drained and exhausted each time? You also have a feeling of dread when you know when they are popping around; the very thought exhausts you. What happened is that your friend or a family member has unknowingly plugged into your energy field and transferred all their negative energy into you. They walk away feeling energised, having got rid of all that negativity, and you, unfortunately, are left with it, which provides fuel to your self-loathing.

How to ask your Spiritual Family for Protection.

Ask your Spiritual Family to come close and surround you with their protective light. Visualise a ball of pure white light about six inches above your head. As you concentrate on this light, notice it getting brighter and more prominent. Slowly bring this ball of beautiful light down to cover your head, neck, and shoulders. It then moves down your body, wrapping itself around you so that you are completely encased in this divine shield. You may feel a strong presence forming around you, all your senses tingling and becoming sensitive, palms of your hands vibrating, and your third eye may be pulsating.

Set your intention, tell your Angel or Guide that you would

like their protection. Do this each time before you encounter your consuming friend or family member. Notice how light and energised you are after their visit? It does not have to be a white light; I often imagine the ball of energy pink. Choose your own colour.

When feeling vulnerable or scared in a negative situation, you can call upon your Spiritual Family for help, as mentioned before in previous chapters, your Angel can intervene, saving your life.

True Story: White Noise

I worked part-time for social services for a period – every Monday, Tuesday, Thursday, and Friday. I had to travel along the same dual carriageway to get to work and back home.

One Monday, leaving for work around nine thirty a.m., I placed one of my favourite CDs into the stereo and turned the volume up. Travelling at the speed limit of 50mph along the empty dual carriageway, listening and singing to the tunes, I was on autopilot, I was oblivious to the road works that had just commenced.

Suddenly my stereo blasted loudly with the sound of piercing crackles and a fussy noise known as white noise, which made me jump out of my skin with pure fright, but more alarmingly, I could not help but scream. Slamming my brakes on, I prayed to myself, 'please don't let me crash.' I skidded forward with my foot firmly on to the brakes and begged the car to stop.

The road works had changed the lanes around, the road I usually travel in was a through road, and the adjoining slip road had to give way, but today the slip road had the right of way, and it was me who had to give way.

A large black BMW jeep with bull bars rightfully joined my

lane, probably thinking I was going to stop. As I heard my tyres screeching, I knew for sure I was going to collide with it.

Holding my breath, I managed to stop inches from it. With my heart pounding so loudly and sweat pouring from my brow, my whole body shook, I had a lucky escape.

Switching off my stereo, I had a feeling that someone above was looking out for me, it was the first and last time the stereo had made this sound, and if it were not for the white noise snapping me out of my trance, ploughing into that big beefy BMW at 50mph would have had severe consequences.

I would like to say thank you to my lovely Angel who had helped me, maybe you had a similar experience where your Angel had intervened?

You can ask your Spiritual Family for their protection to help us shield ourselves from draining and negative people. As mentioned in Animals Spirits, we can call upon them to help us when we feel threatened, our Guides can also help to protect us, sometimes crossing the line by punching your opponent in the face, but there are times when we feel threatened by some other dark force.

Unfortunately, there are good and bad people, it is the same in the spirit world, yes, we do get evil spirits. I have come across them in my time, and I have helped others get rid of them. If you feel threatened at all, ask your Spiritual Family for their protection as well as Archangel Michael and the Hindu goddess Kali. This beautiful goddess is a mighty warrior who hunts and kills all demons. Kali is a force to be wreaking with, there have been a few times that I have called for her help alongside Archangel Michael, they appeared instantly, vanquishing the negative energy.

Some spiritual people do not ask for protection as they feel their Spiritual Family will always protect them. That may be the case, but I have experienced the darkness not because they did not want me to protect me, but because they wanted me to learn and grow from it so I could relate and help others.

True Story: Girl's Trip

I went on a girl's trip with four of my friends, we headed off to Devon, where we stayed in a quaint, beautiful little bed and breakfast. As there were five of us, it was me who stayed in a room by myself. I did not tell the others as I did not want to alarm them, but my room's energy was haunting, which made me shiver. I was not looking forwards to bedtime, I felt afraid to be alone in the room. Sitting on my bed in the pitch dark, feeling uneasy, I knew for sure I would not get an ounce of sleep, I closed my eyes and ask for my Spiritual Family, naming each one if they could protect me. I laid down and rested my head on the pillow and closed my eyes. The next thing I knew, I could hear the birds singing, I could feel the warmth of the sun shining through the window. I could not believe it; it was morning already. Opening my eyes, I had two massive white male lions, lying on each side of me, they had beautiful warming brown and golden eyes. As I regained my focus, the lions faded away. I was thrilled and thankful for their protection.

I have talked about your Angels, Guides, Spirit Animal, there are many more beautiful light beings walking with you, like your grandmother, father, sister, and beloved pets.

Connecting and follows the signs allowing synchronicity to flow through our lives makes us more grounded and understanding of the bigger picture. Once your spiritual connections grow, you will know the word LOVE is the answer to everything and loving yourself is one of your life purposes.

183

"When I loved myself enough, I began leaving whatever wasn't healthy.

This meant people, jobs, my own beliefs, and habits—anything that kept me small.

My judgment called it disloyal. Now I see it as self-loving."
Kim McMill

Grounding Yourself

Grounding is an essential factor, especially when things are hectic, your emotions all over the place, you do not know whether you are coming or going, you are going through a breakup or bereavement, or you have experienced something traumatic. Grounding yourself balances your spiritual and physical energy in your body by connecting you with mother earth. When you are grounded, you feel like you are here: in the physical, in the present. Grounding yourself is especially good for your soul, which enables your self-care and love.

When You Are Not Grounded You May Feel:
> Lightheaded
> Tired
> Disconnected
> Dazed
> Away with the fairies
> Shaky
> Flighty
> Indecisive
> Fearful
> Self-loathing

Grounding yourself can also help your soul get rid of these symptoms and "plug" you back into Mother Earth, balancing your energy and getting you back in touch with your physical body.

How To Ground Yourself

Visualise a ball of white energy on the top of your head.

This ball of energy is going to move down right through your body, as it moves down it collects all the negative energy that your body and your aura are already holding. So, imagining that the ball of energy is like a magnet, move that ball of energy down through your head and into your neck. Gather all the negative energy to the magnetic ball of energy. Continue the power down through the upper body, and into the lower body, absorbing the negative energy as the energy ball moves downwards – into the legs and down into the feet. When the energy reaches the feet, visualise roots growing deep into the earth. The negative energy is then going to be discharged into the ground, where it will be neutralised.

Once all the negativities have been released, grow the roots further downwards, anchoring into Mother Earth's precious crystal.

These roots will draw up positive sparkling white energy. Draw the white energy up through the roots and into the soles of your feet.

Visualise that pure white energy moving up through your legs and into the lower body. Moving upwards to the upper body, then into the neck and head.

Ask then that the energy be used in whatever part of your body, mind, aura that this energy is needed.

Use this little meditation you can tailor to meet your preferences, why not record it on your phone or another device to help you flow through it. An alternative, tune into YouTube, and do one of my favourites: Jason Stephenson Grounding Meditation.

Meditation

Meditations are essential regarding your wellbeing and spiritual connection. If you feel frustrated or angry, it is always good to do meditation even if you do not want to. After the meditation, you will feel completely different, you will no longer hold onto the horrible negative emotions, you will feel lighter, a sensation of relief, you might have some clarity. I would strongly advise you to find time to do one meditation a day and class this as part of your self-care package for yourself.

You can do all different types of mediations as mentioned in previous chapters, you can meditate from one min to hours, it all depends on you. You can get free guided meditations on YouTube and other social media platforms, experiment with them, and find the ones you like.

You do not have to do guided meditations, there is free meditation music that you can simply listen to and let your mind go.

A part of your self-care package is to try and do one cleansing Chakra meditations once a week, which will help eliminate the negative energy clogged in your chakras.

Meditating is such a powerful way to still our minds in chaos and madness, it helps you to bring your attention back to "now."

What is more extraordinary, your thoughts are more powerful than your actions. A collective group of one million children in Thailand meditated for world peace, the remarkable results lower world crime rates for twenty-four – forty-eight hours.

When Australia was on fire, a group of a hundred people or so went to Glastonbury and all mediated at the Tor to help Australia put out the fires. After the meditation, that day in Australia was the first time it started to rain.

If you can try and participate in global meditations, Jason Shurka and Lorie Ladd on Facebook, YouTube and Instagram often do a global meditation to help the world.

Or why not get a group of friends to sit on the beach and do a meditation together? I often do this with friends and send healing, love to them, and we all send beautiful thoughts out to the world.

A note from Running Bear

The goal of meditation is that you become your true self.

Stillness of your mind your soul will speak to you.

Remember magical energy surrounds you, meditation makes your senses sharper and enhance your abilities to tune into these beautiful frequencies.

Try doing a mediation every day.

Self-Care Package

In your journal, design your own self-care package, you can write a list of your dreams, desires, goals, and self-improvements. These can be done on a daily, weekly, or monthly basis. Design a little rota for yourself. You can stick post it notes around your home with beautiful affirmations telling you that you are beautiful, important, worthy etc. You can add a rota or more quotes or set appointments with yourself on your phone if you are a busy bee.

Here are some pointers to help you, it does not matter it is not the same you can add different things.

Daily:

➢ Accept help from others, even though it feels bizarre at first. You cannot do everything alone.

➢ Ask for help from your Spiritual Family.

➢ Watch out for signs, as your Spiritual Family are helping you.

➢ Speak to your loved ones in spirit.

➢ Be aware of how synchronicity presents itself to you in a miraculous way.

➢ Stop trying to please or impress people. Start putting yourself first as you are vital.

➢ Try and do a meditation each day, if only for a few minutes.

➢ Practice the word No, if you do not want to give that lift, or work overtime, or look after someone's else child you do not have to, you have a choice, plus you do not owe them any explanation. No is suffice.

➢ Set some healthy boundaries especially with friend family, colleagues who constantly take and take from you. Once again, start practising no and stop apologising for things that are out of your control.

➢ Do some exercise, you do not have to go to the gym, you can go for a nice walk in the park or the beach.

➢ Do something each day for you, reading a book, go for a walk, hot bubble bath, or do nothing.

➢ Treat yourself like dear old friend.

➢ Try and do one kindness each day, whether it is for you, a friend or animal.

➢ Practice trying to drop your ugly stick.

➢ Practice forgiving yourself.

➢ Watch out for beautiful new beings coming into your life to help you.

➢ Work with your crystals.

➢ Make sure you are getting plenty of rest and sleep, make a routine for yourself and stick to it.

Weekly:

➢ Have a treat every now and then, maybe go out to lunch with family or friends or go for an ice-cream.

➢ Have fun, set aside time for yourself, and do something you love, or go for drink with an old friend reminiscing the good old days, or try something new and outside your comfort zone.

➢ Dress yourself that you feel good in or treat yourself to something new, instead of normal comfy clothes, this will lift your energy up, and make you feel good about yourself, valuing your self-worth.

> Make time for a friend date, being a busy bee all the time, spending quality time with a good friend is healing for your soul.

> Continue to write in your journal your thoughts, feelings, and your discoveries.

> Start by forgiving yourself, reflect on your past mistake and show yourself some kindness, this will help with your self-worth, that you are a beautiful kind being.

> Cleanse your Chakras.

> Use candles or incense stick to cleanse the energy in your environment.

> Use white sage, cleanse you home after negative family and friends have visited, or even if you had bad news.

> Keep doing the exercises within this book.

Monthly

> Treat yourself, get your hair cut, go for a manicure, go for a massage.

> Have a healing treatment, such as reflexology, reiki, Indian head massage etc.

> Global meditation.

Crystal Healing

The use of crystals come from Ancient Sumerians, who included crystals in magical formulas. Since then, people have been attracted to crystals for burial rites, divination practices, healing rituals, spiritual advancement, and even decoration to connote power.

Crystals are a beautiful gift provided by Mother Earth to help us heal in so many ways. Some crystals help heal old wounds in your heart, allowing love to flow freely through you, helping you start loving yourself. Some crystal helps you to speak your truth with dignity and grace, others will protect you. There are so many different beautiful, powerful crystals that will make a massive difference if you open your heart to them.

One of the fantastic things about crystals they will choose you, I have been blessed, I have been given crystals over the years as I was so drawn to them, and they have magically helped me.

True Story: My Smokey Quartz Sphere
A spiritual friend of mine recommended that I ought to obtain a crystal called Smokey Quartz. She also foretold that on the path ahead of me I would be surrounded by a lot of negativities. Some people from the spiritual society will be envious and jealous that I was naturally gifted; hence this crystal would protect me from negative energy. The next day, following her advice, I went to a crystal shop. I did not have much money, but I thought I could

pick up a crystal for less than £10.

On entering the shop, a strong sensation overwhelmed me; it was as though I was being drawn to something, it was so powerful. Letting myself go I was pulled over to the locked display cabinet, my eyes fixated on a small sphere.

"That has just picked you!" An elderly man came out from behind his counter and walked towards me.

"What?" I said in disbelief.

"You don't choose a crystal, they choose you!" He smiled.

Glancing back at the crystal I winced. How could that be? It was priced at fifty pounds; there was no way I could afford it. The man unlocked the cabinet and placed the sphere into my hands. It felt so right; I wanted it, but how? The man must have seen the distress in my face.

"How much have you got?"

I explained to him that I wanted to get a crystal for £10 or less and my eyes drifted off to the smaller, cheaper crystals as I handed back the sphere.

"No, I can't take it back, it wants you!"

Again, I felt my body wince; I did not want to give up the beautiful crystal sphere but there was no way I could afford it! Being a full-time student and single mum to five children, I could not afford luxuries such as this.

"I will take ten pounds for it!"

"No, you can't!"

Quickly doing the maths, there was no profit in it for him; he was probably giving it to me for less than it cost him.

"You can feel the magnetism?"

"Yes, it's wonderful, it's so strong!"

"I'm not taking 'no' for an answer. Give me ten pounds and it's yours!" He was adamant.

I was astounded by his generosity and kindness.

"If you keep it close by, it will look after you!"

I could not thank him enough. Taking my Smokey Quartz Sphere home, I knew exactly where I could keep it – on top of my dressing table would be the perfect spot.

True Story: Alarm

A couple of months later after purchasing my Smokey Quartz Sphere, coming home from church on one dark, cold, Tuesday night I was adamant I was not alone. At church I recently joined a close circle. I had seen a lot of spirits and had mostly wonderful experiences with them. Naively I thought everyone in the circle had seen or felt spirit. I was shocked and alarmed when most of them hardly had any experiences at all. The medium, Jane, conducted the circle and she instantly took me under her wing. She seemed pleasant enough, but I felt it a bit daunting having my mentor grabbing me at every session demanding that I should tell her future. I was embarrassed each time she sang my praises to the group whilst she would put others down. I could see on some of their faces that they disapproved of me. One woman, who was named Sue, was in her late forties and would often brag to me. She told me she had been in the circle for years and that she had met Colin Fry who told her she was an amazing medium. She would try to impress Jane, offering her a reading which she always turned down. According to Jane, I was the golden girl who infuriated Sue.

Walking to the car I could have sworn someone was following me. Repeatedly, I kept looking over my shoulder as my feet picked up the pace. I quickly got into the car, locked all the doors and I felt safer. Driving home I had a horrible feeling someone was in the back seat. Every time I glanced in the rear-

194

view mirror for a brief second, I could see a black silhouette. I drove fast as my heart pounded and I could not wait to get home. I jumped out of the car and, quickly locking it, I ran indoors and secured the front door.

"Hi, Mum!"

I jumped out of my skin. It was Elisha.

"You, OK?" she asked.

"Yeah, I'm fine! I didn't see you there!" I replied, holding my heart in place.

"What was church like?"

"Yeah, it was good." I smiled at her.

I did not want to frighten her; brushing off the ordeal, I put it down to my overactive imagination playing tricks on me. I had a cup of tea with Elisha; the rest of the children were in bed, and I felt much calmer. Having wound myself up like that, I felt exhausted and told my daughter of sixteen years of age, I was going to have an early night. I retired into my warm luxurious waterbed and heard Elisha climb her ladder – I had converted the loft into a bedroom for her. As I lay there, I could hear her getting into bed.

"Goodnight, Mum!" she called softly.

"Goodnight Babes, sweet dreams!" I softly called back.

I closed my eyes and felt my body relaxing. I felt a complete fool that I had spooked myself and I softly giggled.

Suddenly I heard a tinkling noise, it sounded like drops of water dropping onto to a crystal glass. I bolted up in bed as a horrifying thought raced through my mind. Was there a water leak in Elisha's room? Was the water coming through my light bulb? Getting out of bed, logic started to creep in. It was not raining, but where was this water coming from?

I nervously switched on my light and examined my light

bulb. There was no evidence of a leak. This puzzled me, where was this noise coming from?

"Mum, what's that noise?" softly shouted Elisha.

"You can hear it?"

"Yeah, what is it?"

"I don't know!"

Looking around the room, I was determined to find out where this noise was coming from. I closed my eyes and followed my ears. I could not believe it.

"Oh my god!" I gasped.

"What Mum, what is it?" Elisha sounded startled.

"You're not going to believe it!" I said, putting my ear up to it.

"The tinkling noise is coming from my Smokey Quart Sphere."

"What?" Lilly was astounded.

I picked up the sphere and the noise instantly stopped. Giving it a loving stroke, I was bewildered; was it trying to tell me something? I replaced my sphere, switched off the light and jumped back into bed.

"Why was it making a noise?" Elisha asked.

"I'm not sure… it's spooky… anyway, I'm going to sleep now… goodnight, Babes," I softly shouted.

"OK. Goodnight, Mum!"

Closing my eyes, I could not help but wonder at this strange night. I drifted off to sleep but suddenly I was awoken violently, an almighty force came crashing down onto my chest; I felt hands around my neck; for a split second I thought someone had broken in and was strangling me. I opened my eyes so wide they were almost popping out of their sockets with fright but there was nothing there. I was paralysed but my body moved aggressively with the tidal wave of the bed.

"Mum! Are you all right?" screamed Elisha.

I could hear something hissing into my face. Suddenly I broke free from its grip; I was gasping for air, my heart almost exploding out of my chest. I have never seen my bedroom look so dark. I knew it was in the darkest shadows waiting to pounce on me again. I had never been so scared in my life.

"Yeah, I'm OK!" My voice trembled with fear.

"Dad, Nan, Granddad, my Angels and those in spirit that come in the name of love and light please protect my children, please protect me. Get rid of it, Dad?" I quietly prayed.

I huddled up with the duvet, there was no way that I could go back to sleep. Staying awake all night my brain worked overtime. I knew for sure my faithful Smokey Quartz Sphere acted as an alarm. I was not imagining it when I thought something was following me home. Had someone from the church sent me this? But why? Did they want to frighten me off? Who would do such a thing? Was it Sue?

Whatever it was, by the following day it was gone. At the next meeting, I took my mentor Jane to one side and tried telling her about my experience. First, I had to tell her whether she was going to lose her job; shutting my eyes I was told YES. She was not happy with my answer and sort of dismissed it. When I finally told her, what had happened she told me not to worry about it, in fact she was pleased I had experienced a negative spirit; at least now, when working with them, I could tell the difference.

This beautiful crystal that I cherish and adore has gone off like an alarm several times since. Now, I know the meaning behind it, so I asked for protection from my Spiritual Family, and I immediately feel safe.

Crystals are rocks that carry beautiful energy. They are

provided for us by the Earth to help us heal, so we must respect and take care of them.

Crystals absorb our energy when we hold them and the energy around them, like a sponge with water. Therefore, you must cleanse & recharge them as the crystal will stop working once it is overloaded.

One of my favourite ways to cleanse and charge my crystals is by leaving them on my windowsill under the full moon. My friends leave hers in her back garden for the night. In the morning, you will find your crystal all sparkly and infused with moon energy. Another favourite of mine to cleanse and charge my crystals is using my singing bowl and letting the vibrations go through the crystals.

You can use your lovely crystals during meditation, they will help guide and inspire you. You can decoratively place them in any room, and if you have tumble stones, you can pop them in your pockets or purse/wallet. Wearing crystals as jewellery is another favourite way to work with them. If I am anxious about an appointment or any other situation, I will wear one of my crystal bracelets that I am drawn to. Start today and work with the magical essence of your crystal.

The Magic of This Book

My self-love journey has been extremely challenging. Life throws unexpecting obstacles in your way, staying positive all the time is such a hard concept to achieve. Even though I use the tools to help me get through life's obstacle course, there are moments when I, too, have lapses where I feel sadness and despair. This is normal, as I am only human. I have come to this earth to experience all human emotions, but during these lapses, even though I do not pick up my ugly stick, I still feel flat and weary.

The magic of this book, even though I am the author, I have experienced this phenomenon on many occasions.

Each time when I have these dark lapses, I pick this book up and randomly pick a page, even though I know this book inside out. I am surprised, the text lifting off the page generates my soul, making me feel energised and sparkling, the words of wisdom send healing rays to my heart, making me feel joy and happiness. I close the book, and I am grateful for this wonderful experience.

Once you have read this book, keep it close to hand, in your handbag, on the side dresser in your bedroom, etc. When you have your lapse, do not be hard on yourself, you are human full of beautiful emotions, sadness is part of your experience, and it is okay to feel this way, but if your sadness turns into days, try this method. Randomly pick a page, you will be amazed.

True Story: The End
One sunny morning sitting in the living room, with the laptop sat

on my lap, I was writing the last chapter for this book. Working on the last paragraph, I was so excited to nearly have my book completed when suddenly a large flying thing flew into my face and jittered in front of the screen. I was just about to give it a back hander when I realised what it was. I froze to the spot. I could not believe my eyes as I watched a big orb, the size of a man's fist, bouncing in front of the screen. I was thrilled and ecstatic – it too seemed to share my excitement.

"Do you mind, may I continue?" I spoke to the over excited orb.

List of All Exercises

Exercise 1 "Fighting your inner demons"
This exercise can help you fight these demons (cruel experiences). Find a quiet place, think of a negative experience in your past, try and go to your earliest memory.

For example: Maybe you came last in a race, and your parent or teacher were disappointed with you. Think of how you felt at that moment. I bet you tried your best, but it was not good enough for them. For a moment, you are the adult addressing the small child (you). What would you say to that little child? Would you scold him/her? Would you be mean to him/her? The answer would be NO, you would not. What kind of words would you say? Speak to them out loud. Shower that small child with love and healing, give him/her a loving hug. You may have to repeat this several times, over a short period, have patients.

Exercise 2 "Dear Old Friend"
When your dear friend is around at yours crying upon your shoulder, telling you all about her woes, are you cold or unpleasant to her? Do you stamp on her when she is down? No, you do not. You show her kindness, love, and support. From now on, you need to start treating yourself like a dear old friend. When you have a negative thought about yourself, ask yourself, would you say this to your friend? Would you tell her that she was fat, ugly, useless, etc.? When you feel negative about yourself, say some kind, loving words. Speak to yourself in your head or out

loud, show yourself some compassion. If you cannot do this, write down in your journal your disturbing thoughts.

Now pretend your friend had written this about herself. Write underneath some thoughtful and nurturing words that you would say to your dear friend, keep repeating this, it does not matter that you are pretending as for one day you will start believing in yourself, start this today.

Exercise 3 "Your Positives"

I find most people find showing themselves kindness and love treating themselves as a dear friend is a hard concept, as they are suffering from low self-esteem and are full of self-loathing. I asked them to name ten positives about themselves, which they all struggle to answer one or two.

When I asked them to name ten negatives, without hesitation, they reel off a long list. I, too, was like this, and I found it hard to say anything positive about me as I clung to my ugly stick. Most of us have at least one loving person in our life that shows us kindness, whether it is a daughter, friend, or spouse. For the first time, do not be afraid to ask for help. Ask them if they could help you make a list of all your positives, you will be pleasantly surprised how people perceive you. When you make your negative list, they will shock you, they will tell you that you do not believe in yourself, you are extremely hard on yourself, and you lack confidence. These comments will be completely different from your negative list, as yours will be cruel and harsh, whereas theirs are not negatives, they are your challenges that you will overcome with time. Write this all down in your journal, and your list will end up looking like this:

My Positives
- I am kind.
- I am caring.
- I am a good mother.
- I am a good wife.
- I am a good friend.
- I have a big loving heart.
- I make excellent cakes and so on.

My Challenges
- To be more confident.
- To love me and put myself first.
- To believe in myself, I do matter.
- To learn how to say No.
- To drop my Ugly Stick and show myself some kindness, and so on.

Have this list where you can see this most day, on your vanity mirror, fridge, or mobile.

If you have a moment where you cannot drop your Ugly Stick, pick up your list, and read your positives. Over time, you will start to believe in yourself.

Exercise 4 "YOU!"
Use this little exercise every time you start too self-loath. Find a peaceful spot, your bedroom, garden, or sitting in your car.

Take a deep breath in and exhale slowly, do this twice more. Just for a moment, bring your attention to your breathing, it may seem bizarre at first. At this moment, ask yourself, what makes you happy? What are your passions? What is your dream? What would you like to do? Maybe at first, you do not know that all you want is to be happy and feel peace and harmony. If you are finding difficulties, confide in a good friend who will listen and support you.

Get them to help you write in your journal a little to-do list. Once you have completed it, make sure you check it off your list and note how it made you feel, it does not have to be a long sentence, just one or two words will do.

- Get my hair cut – I look so much better
- Go for a massage – I feel so relaxed
- Go for a walk in the forest – I felt free
- Sit by the beach – I love watching the waves, I felt peaceful
- Have a relaxing bath – I can feel all my tension and stress evaporating.

The aim is to change the way you think, stop beating yourself up, and bring attention to your true self.

Exercise 5 "No"

Another little exercise to help those who always give in, is to practice in front of a mirror, if you are uncomfortable with that, find a quiet little place, bedroom, garden, and practice saying "No" out loud.

Believe it or not, this little word changes the vibrations in your aura, making you feel more energetic, worthy, and you do matter.

Exercise 6 "Sorry"

Try for one day, count how many times you say the word "Sorry." Write down in a journal what prompted you to say it.

Have two columns, was it in your control or out of your

control. If you made a mistake, i.e., Put sugar in your friend's tea when they do not have sugar, that would be in your control, hence it is a valid "Sorry." Out of your control, i.e., your partner has misplaced his razor and accuses you of taking it. This is not the case, but you are full of apologies and help him to find it.

He finds it and remembers that he did place it in a different location. You are feeling relieved, but how many times did you say "Sorry"?

Control Sorry	Qty	Out of your Control Sorry	Qty
Sugar in friend's tea	1	misplace razor blamed me	7

Writing in your journal will provide you with clarity. When you start to ask yourself questions, you will open your eyes, sparking many revelations.

Why do you have to be sorry if he misplaced his razor?

You know you never touch it, why did you say sorry for something you never did?

Why are you sorry for his bad behaviour towards you?

Keep updating your journal, and in time the column 'Out of your Control Sorry' will vanish.

Exercise 7 "Anger"

When a negative situation arises, and you feel angry towards it, ask yourself, who does it hurt?

Write in your journal of your feelings, this is important as you will discover, holding onto this anger, you are only hurting yourself.

Ask yourself another question, do you deserve to feel this way?

Write some kind words, treat yourself like a dear friend, send love to yourself, and send positive healing thoughts to the person who has upset you. It may be hard at first, but by sending them love and healing out, you are letting go of your anger.

Exercise 8 "Forgiveness"
Running Bear told me to write myself a little note, it can be in your journal, mobile, iPad, etc. Go back to a pain that you hold onto, in this instant, when my home was repossessed. First, accept the past, you cannot change it. Write down how you felt, and in the second column, treat yourself like a dear friend, as mentioned in the previous chapter.

Shameful	You were so brave.
Judged	You are a wonderful, beautiful being.
Belittled	You would never treat anyone like this.
Failure	You have come so far, I am so proud.
Wanted to die	I am elated that you are alive.

I FORGIVE MYSELF – I FORGIVE MYSELF – I FORGIVE MYSELF

If you need help with this, ask a dear friend to help you. Read this little note to yourself for twenty-one days straight, these lovely comments in the second column will start to wash the pain from your soul. Some of you may need longer, so I recommend thirty days. Write in your journal how you felt before this exercise and after, you will see a huge difference. You can repeat this exercise as many times as you want, each time, there will be a difference. Remember, it is not a race or a competition, I had to repeat this task a few times over two years. The human soul is like an onion with layers and layers, it is not an overnight fix, take your time, and you will get there.

Exercise 9 "Spirit Guides"

Feeling all out of sorts – not too sure why?

Maybe this week, you start your driving lessons.

In this example, your main Guide has got you a new teacher to help you with your driving lessons.

Feeling sad, feels as though you are missing someone, but no one has left?

You have just finished your last exam, Yippee.

In this example, the Guide who helped you with your revision and exams has completed his task, he is no longer needed.

Take note in your journal of these feelings and ask yourself what is going on in your life?

Exercise 10 "Who is my Guide?"

Write down what you are drawn to in your journal, there may be a list, that is okay. Try some meditations, it may take time, so please be patient. Keep all your findings written down in your journal, you will notice a pattern forming. Ask yourself, do you feel a woman or male presence? The first thing that pops into your head is the answer, this is your Guide communicating with you. Keep asking questions, you can even ask for a name. I have known people to connect with their Guide first time only to doubt and dismiss everything. So, you need to have faith and belief.

Dreams are significant, this is the best way your guide and loved ones in spirit can communicate with you. Write your vision down in your journal, you may not understand it now but give it time to become a revelation. If you have any concerns or worries, it is good to ask for help.

Exercise 11 "Communicate with your Guides"

This simple meditation technique is an extremely excellent way to let your Guides communicate with you. You can meditate for one minute, five minutes, or however long you want. This is the meditation I had been doing, and after several times of doing it, Running Bear materialised right beside me.

Many people tend to find it hard to meditate as constant thoughts randomly interrupt their peace. They are trying too hard to concentrate on nothing and find it annoying when reminded that they are out of milk or sugar. This is the monkey brain that chitters and chatters, so all you need to do is quieten it.

To quieten the monkey brain, all you need to do is give it a task, such as telling it to concentrate on breathing.

Breathe in… Breathe out…
Breathe in… Breathe out…
Breathe in… Breathe out…
Just simply be aware of your breath.

Exercise 12 "Who is my Animal Spirit?"

Write down in your journal what animal do you love the most? Then do a meditation with your guide, or you can do a guided meditation with Jason Stephenson, "meet your animal spirit" on YouTube. Again, write down in your journal your discoveries.

Exercise 13 "Why do I Hate myself?"

In your journal, write down, why do you hate yourself?

Look a little bit deeper, where did it come from? Has someone said this to you? If so, would you consider them a nice person? When they said it, were they angry? What is their background? What are their fears? Keep asking yourself more questions.

For example:

I hate myself because I am fat.

Where did it come from?

I have just had a baby.

I feel insecure about my weight and body.

My husband keeps on about my weight.

My husband says horrible things to me, I consider him to be mean.

My husband was not angry when he says it, he likes to say it to me as he knows it upsets me.

He has loving parents, but he is the only child. He likes to get his own way, and he tends to be selfish. He is afraid of being alone.

Once you have written it down, get a dearly trusted friend to look at your list. Having a different perspective can shed new light on the matter, which can give you a significant epiphany.

Write underneath your list your findings.

Example: I have discovered that I am not fat, I am beautiful and proud to be me, my husband is so scared of losing me that he is going to the extreme extent to make me feel like rubbish, to make him feel better. I do not deserve to be treated this way. I ask for healing for him and myself.

Keep documenting your feelings, insecurities, and fears. Open your mind and question every aspect of their origins. Where did this come from? Why did this happen? Etc.

Take note each time you felt low, what happened around you. Reading this book has started or advancing your awakening, you are now more susceptible of feeling, hearing, and seeing the beautiful magic all around you. Take note each time you felt low, what happened around you. I bet something amazing happened, just lift up your chin and you will be able to see.

Do not forget to design your self-care plan

Recap Benefits of Loving Yourself

No one is perfect, and we all have flaws, loving yourself unconditionally will lead you to accept and love all your mistakes, regrets, weaknesses, and all.

I Love Me is about owning your power within and showing yourself love and kindness.

Allowing the love to flow through you makes you less likely to let bad habits and abusive relationships to block your way, forming a new positive change in your life.

As you begin your journey to loving yourself unconditionally, your life will automatically fall into place. You will possess the power to design your life around events that make you happy.

Here are some benefits why I Love Me is essential.

Acceptance

Acceptance is recognizing all your positive and negatives qualities, showering each one with Love, and allowing peace and harmony into your heart.

Recommended crystals to help you on your journey:
- ➢ Blue Lace Agate – Communication
- ➢ Black Tourmaline – Protection
- ➢ Orac Agate – Go with the Flow – Healing – Forgiveness
- ➢ Rose Quartz – Love – Love yourself – Fertility – Healing

Self-Awareness

Self-awareness brings to light all your strengths, weakness, your aspirations, and dreams, which will give you a better understanding of yourself, giving you a clear direction.

Recommended crystals:

➢ Chevron Amethyst – Spiritual – Protection – Best version of yourself

➢ Larimar – Communication – Finding your path – Healing

➢ Sunset Aura Quartz – Joy – Let Go – Positivity

➢ Tiger Eye – Good luck – Success – Protection – Working with the universe

Mind, Body and Soul

Loving yourself does wonder for your whole wellbeing. Showing yourself love is like watering a flower, taking care of it, and showing it kindness, you will bloom like a beautiful flower. You will reap beautiful rewards of health, peace, and success in your world.

Recommended crystals:

➢ Amethyst – Tranquillity – Spiritual wisdom – Protection

➢ Mangano Calcite – Self-love – Healing

➢ Moss Agate – New beginnings – Believe in yourself – Healing – Success – Self-esteem

➢ Prasiolite Quartz – Success – Prosperity – Abundance – Healing

Respect

Once we are on our self-love journey, respect is one of the first emotions that bounces back to us, empowering your worthiness and happiness. This strong emotion will be one of the main driving forces to help you on your journey.

Recommended crystals:

➢ Aura Rose Quartz – Romance – Love for yourself –

Finding yourself

> Blue Goldstone – Confidence – Opportunities – Stand in your power – Healing
> Morganite – New love – Healing heart
> Septarian – Grounding – Patients – Protection

Competence

As your self-love increases, you will realise the only person you need to please is yourself. You will no longer look for that agonizing perfection or a terrible mistake. You will appreciate that doing your best is enough, which will empower your competence.

Recommended crystals:

> Banded Agate – Good Luck – Wealth – Healing
> Blue Goldstone – Confidence – Opportunities – Stand in your power – Healing
> Blue Kyanite – Trusting yourself – Psychic ability – Dreaming
> Dendritic Agate – Peace – Confidence – Protection – Abundance – Prosperity

Confidence

Confidence takes time to grow but showing yourself love, you will bloom; the feeling of worthless and all your insecurities will fade and be replaced with strength, you will value all of yourself accepting your faults and being okay with it. You will adopt a healthy attitude, no one is perfect. I will just do my best.

Recommended crystals:

> Blue Lace Agate – Communication
> Morganite – New love – Healing heart
> Sodalite – Spiritual Growth – Believe in yourself – Helps

grief

> Sunset Aura Quartz – Joy – Let Go – Positivity

Comfort in your own skin

I find that being happy in your own skin is the one most people struggle with, but with time on your self-love journey, you will be able to embrace and love every part of you. There is only one of you in this world, and you will realise how special you are.

Recommended crystals:

> Aura Rose Quartz – Romance – Love for yourself – Finding yourself

> Mangano Calcite – Self-love – Healing

> Pink Opal – Love – Healing the heart – Releasing old wounds

> Rose Quartz – Love – Love yourself – Fertility – Healing

Fearless

On your self-love journey, you will discover the magical word love is the most potent force in the universe. You will have the ability to replace fear with love, which will evolve you into a fearless, beautiful being.

Recommended crystals:

> Angelite – Angels – Spirit – Protection – Spiritual Growth

> Pink Opal – Love – Healing the heart – Releasing old wounds

> Pyrite – Protection – Foresight – Trusting the universe

> Unakite – Healing – Grounding – Now – Dreams

Competition and Jealousy

When we love ourselves, we let go of the notion of keeping up with the Joneses. We stop comparing ourselves to others, eliminating jealousy and enviousness.

You will believe that you are an incredible version of the true you.

Recommended crystals:

➢ Black Obsidian – Protection – Healing – Communication
➢ Black Tourmaline – Protection
➢ Fluorite – Helps the mind – Grounding – In the now
➢ Aquamarine – Healing – Courage – Judgmentalism

Let Go

Letting go at the beginning of your self-love journey can be one of the most challenging obstacles to overcome, but as you allow the love to flow freely, you will discover letting go of the old baggage that you carry with you, no longer serves you. The more you release, the more you will grow, inviting infinite opportunities.

Recommended crystals:

➢ Orac Agate – Go with the Flow – Healing – Forgiveness
➢ Sunset Aura Quartz – Joy – Let Go – Positivity
➢ Tiger Eye – Good luck – Success – Protection – Working with the universe
➢ Unakite – Healing – Grounding – Now – Dreams

Believing in Yourself

When you start to believe in yourself, something magical happens to you.

All your dreams, passions, desires become a possibility. You will discover that you are the master of your own universe, where anything is possible.

Recommended crystals:

➢ Blue Kyanite – Trusting yourself – Psychic ability –

Dreaming
- Blue Goldstone – Confidence – Opportunities – Stand in your power – Healing
- Moss Agate – New beginnings – Believe in yourself – Healing – Success – Self-esteem
- Sodalite – Spiritual Growth – Believe in yourself – Helps grief

Healing Empathy

Loving yourself, changes your whole wellbeing, evolving you into your true self, you will be bestowed with vast knowledge and understanding. You will have the power to sense and feel others' emotions, helping them to commence on their self-love journey.

Recommended crystals:
- Lapis lazuli – Healing headaches – Spiritual enlightenment – Improving relationships
- Morganite – New love – Healing heart
- Red Howlite – Emotions – Nurture relationships with females – Spiritual growth
- Rose Quartz – Love – Love yourself – Fertility – Healing

You Radiate

On your journey, you will discover it does not matter what other people think of you, it is how you feel about yourself that is important. This boosts your confidence, which will enable you to love every part of you, embracing the imperfections and accepting them as beautiful. You will naturally shine.

Recommended crystals:
- Angelite – Angels – Spirit – Protection – Spiritual Growth
- Opalite – Communication – Persistent – Love

➢ Labradorite – Spiritual Growth – Magic – Trust in spirit

➢ Moss Agate – New beginnings – Believe in yourself – Healing – Success – Self-esteem

Law of Attraction

When you start to love yourself, you change the magnetic fields around you to positives. The more you grow, embracing the love, the more likely you will attract positivity and love you want into your life.

Recommended crystals:

➢ Blue Kyanite – Trusting yourself – Psychic ability – Dreaming

➢ Merlinite – Magic – Self-discovery – Spiritual Growth – Forgiveness

➢ Pyrite – Protection – Foresight – Trusting the universe

➢ Tiger Eye – Good luck – Success – Protection – Working with the universe

Friends & Family

Loving yourself has a severe impact on your relationships with your friends and family, especially those who only take and take from you. They are not going to like the real you as you can say the word proudly, "No." You now value yourself, your time, and your energy.

You will no longer hold onto grudges or be angry at someone for a long time, as you will realise this does you more harm than good. You will be able to forgive those that have hurt you, as you have discovered this is a kindness to you, and all you want is to be happy.

When people leave your life, you are no longer afraid as you have got yourself.

Recommended crystals:

➢ Aura Rose Quartz – Romance – Love for yourself – Finding yourself

➢ Blue Goldstone – Confidence – Opportunities – Stand in your power – Healing

➢ Blue Lace Agate – Communication

➢ Lapis lazuli – Healing headaches – Spiritual enlightenment – Improving relationships

➢ Red Howlite – Emotions – Nurture relationships with females – Spiritual growth

Better Relationships

When we start to love ourselves, you begin to form a low tolerance for people who do not respect you or treat you poorly. You will repel it and adopt an attitude that you do not have time for them.

You will gravitate to people who treat you kindly than those who do not.

Loving yourself, you eliminate jealousy, insecurity, and anger, making way for better relationships.

Recommended crystals:

➢ Lapis lazuli – Healing headaches – Spiritual enlightenment – Improving relationships

➢ Morganite – New love – Healing heart

➢ Red Howlite – Emotions – Nurture relationships with females – Spiritual growth

➢ Rose Quartz – Love – Love yourself – Fertility – Healing

➢ Sunset Aura Quartz – Joy – Let Go – Positivity

World Changes

When you fall in love with yourself, everything around you

changes, life becomes beautiful. You are gifted with a new perspective. You are now able to see the wonderous magic around you. Self-love evolves you into your true self, making you a better person.

You take better care of your physical, psychological, spiritual, and emotional state. You love life as it attracts beautiful people and favourable circumstances in your life.

Recommended crystals:

➢ Labradorite –   Spiritual Growth – Magic – Trust in spirit – Transformation

➢ Opalite – Communication – Persistent – Love – Transformation

➢ Merlinite – Magic – Self-discovery – Spiritual Growth – Forgiveness

➢ Serpentine – Spiritual Connection – Healing

Less Stress, Anxiety, and Depression

When we love ourselves, we react differently to circumstances with a deep feeling of inner peace, instead of reacting, why is this happening? We now ask ourselves, what are our lessons? This removes our fears and worries, thus helping to reduce stress and anxiety.

Loving yourself, you are in good practice of being in the now, no longer depressed with the past, or anxious about the future. You have accepted these dark thoughts no longer serve you.

Recommended crystals:

➢ Angelite – Angels – Spirit – Protection – Spiritual Growth – Reduce Stress

➢ Amethyst – Tranquillity – Spiritual wisdom – Protection – Reduce Stress

➤ Banded Agate – Good Luck – Wealth – Healing – Reduce Stress

➤ Dumortierite – Healing – Headaches – Studying – Reduce Stress

Happiness

Loving yourself, you are going through a significant transformation like a caterpillar blooming into a butterfly. Once you genuinely love yourself and become the butterfly, you will discover that loving yourself is the key to your happiness.

Recommended crystals:

➤ Amethyst – Tranquillity – Spiritual wisdom – Protection

➤ Aura Rose Quartz – Romance – Love for yourself – Finding yourself

➤ Dendritic Agate – Peace – Confidence – Protection – Abundance – Prosperity

➤ Pink Opal – Love – Healing the heart – Releasing old wounds

The World is Your Oyster

Your self-worth improves when you start to love yourself, and with this, you begin to believe in yourself. This is very empowering, making you believe that you can accomplish anything you set your mind to or go anywhere in the world to fulfil your dreams.

Recommended crystals:

➤ Dendritic Agate – Peace – Confidence – Protection – Abundance – Prosperity

➤ Fluorite – Helps the mind – Grounding – In the now

➤ Larimar – Communication – Finding your path – Healing

➤ Sunset Aura Quartz – Joy – Let Go – Positivity

Loneliness

When our self-love improves, our connection to the spiritual world grows. We know that we are never truly on our own as we embrace a deeper relationship with yourself, spending time on your own will not feel scary any more, you will love your own company and that of spirit.

Recommended crystals:

➤ Angelite – Angels – Spirit – Protection – Spiritual Growth

➤ Caribbean Calcite – Communication with spirit

➤ Labradorite – Spiritual Growth – Magic – Trust in spirit

➤ Sodalite – Spiritual Growth – Believe in yourself – Helps grief

Freedom

Self-love unshackles you from all life restraints, you discover nothing can hold you back. You are free to be your fabulous self, you are free to shine your light in this world.

➤ Black Obsidian – Protection – Healing – Communication

➤ Labradorite – Spiritual Growth – Magic – Trust in spirit

➤ Merlinite – Magic – Self-discovery – Spiritual Growth – Forgiveness

➤ Unakite – Healing – Grounding – Now – Dreams

Loving You

You will become your own best friend; you will stop being desperate for a romantic relationship as you will value your time and belief. You will discover that you do not need a partner to be happy. Instead, you will adopt the mindset your happiness is essential, and the right person will show up in time. You will be kinder to yourself and stop beating yourself up. You will embrace your true self and beam a beautiful light into the universe, attracting an abundance of love and goodies for yourself. Your soul will radiate with joy and happiness, transforming your whole world around you.

You will discover the secret key to life is all about loving oneself. With these teachings and many lessons learned, you will be an excellent advocate for spirit, helping others embrace their light.

There are many more benefits that you will discover, just make sure you keep a journal with your findings. One of the things you will surely first discover is that you will be better at prioritizing your own needs before others, which is a marvellous revelation. You will start treating yourself with uplifting gifts and treatments, such as flowers, pedicures, reflexology, etc., which will all strengthen your self-love.

Crystal Glossary

Angelite - Angels - Spirit – Protection - Spiritual Growth
Angelite is a beautiful protection crystal to help protect you from lower energies, dispelling fear, and anxiety. Meditating with it will help you to reduce those uncomfortable feelings that you are holding in your solar plexus and clearing those lower thoughts you have in your mind. It naturally lifts your vibration; it is perfect for you to be creative in whatever way. It helps to express your creativity with a peaceful energy that is calming and soothing.

It enhances your connection to your Angel, Guides, and loved ones in spirit. Angelite helps you to trust their guidance and messages through your consciousness.

Those thoughts you are having, inspiring ideas, are coming from your Angels and Guides. Watch out for their signs, feathers, songs coming onto the radio, or whispers in your ears. They cannot interfere with your free will, but they can assist you in your daily life.

Amethyst - Tranquillity - Spiritual wisdom - Protection
Amethyst is the crystal of tranquillity, if you feel anxious and unsure what lies ahead, this crystal, amethyst, helps alleviate those feelings of anxiety. It brings tranquillity into your whole being, into your mind, and your emotions enabling you to go about your day healthy and happy, and sleeping with it underneath your pillow will soothe your sleep. It raises your

vibration, allowing you to live in a much more harmonious way. Amethyst is also a crystal of spiritual protection and purification. It opens your third eye and crown chakra, helping you connect to your intuition and spiritual wisdom. It is known as the crystal of spirituality.

Aquamarine - Healing - Courage - Judgmentalism

Aquamarine helps you understand your emotions and where they are coming from. What thoughts have created those emotions? It enables you to understand what is causing your stress, what events, incidences, situation, and why you are experiencing them. It brings clarity to your mind and emotions, enabling you to recognise and release any negative thoughts.

It can invoke tolerance of others and overcomes judgmentalism, giving support to those overwhelmed by responsibility.

It is a crystal of courage that can calm you and help eliminate those stresses so you can live in peace.

Aura Rose Quartz - Romance - Love for yourself - Finding yourself

Aura Rose Quartz is a beautiful crystal that attracts love to you and helps you feel a stronger sense of love for yourself. It enhances all the love aspect in your life, i.e., romance, friendship, and life itself… It raises your vibration and vitality and gives you a new sense of purpose, a new sense of direction, a new sense of peace, respect, and tranquillity. Ideal crystal to have when you are single.

Banded Agate - Good Luck - Wealth - Healing

Banded Agate is known as the crystal of calmness, good luck, and wealth. It gently balances your energies, eliminating those lower energies that keep you stuck and those lower energies that create nervousness and anxiety within you. It wants to help you bring you back to love, peace, and tranquillity within yourself.

It gives you strength, stability, and balance to deal with everything going around you when that happens.

Blue Goldstone - Confidence - Opportunities - Stand in your power - Healing

Blue Goldston is a man-made crystal with beautiful properties, it lifts your vitality, and it mainly works on the solar plexus. It helps you to feel more comfortable about who you are. It also boosts your confidence and self-respect, particularly when you feel compromised or made to feel inadequate. It makes you feel vital and positive, especially in what you are doing. It is an excellent crystal for job opportunities and interviews. It will help you stand in your own power. It contains copper and therefore supports healing your joints.

Blue Kyanite - Trusting yourself - Psychic ability - Dreaming

Blue Kyanite is a beautiful crystal to bring light energy into your lives as it naturally lifts you.

It also helps you trust yourself, trust your intuition, and trust the universe responds to you in the way you need it to. It enables you to communicate sincerely and authentically as it resonates with the throat chakra. Blue kyanite has a high vibration and helps open your psychic abilities. If you sleep with one under your pillow, it can help with dreaming. It stimulates your third eye chakra to connect with your Spiritual Family.

It is great to use in spiritual work to clear your energetic field and form a bubble of protection around you.

Blue Lace Agate - Communication

Blue Lace is a crystal of communication and resonates with the throat chakra, it helps you if you have difficulty being heard by others or need confidence and articulation to share your truth. It helps create a sense of unity and harmony within yourself and with those you are communicating with. It can help build community and loyalty amongst family and friends, giving you a sense of belonging.

Black Obsidian - Protection - Healing - Communication
Black Obsidian resonates with the throat chakra and helps you to freely express your thoughts and feeling with clarity. Sometimes you hold back your true feelings and thoughts for fear of hurting whoever you are talking to. You cannot bear to be confrontational. This crystal helps you convey your thoughts and feelings with a loving heart to those you are speaking to.

This crystal wants to bring up past traumas and past hurt that needs to be released and healed. It helps you recognise those traumas' truth and clears any negative thoughts/patterns holding you back. This crystal can help eliminate any negative energy in your room and protect you from negative people and situations and electromagnet fields coming from your computer, etc.

Black Tourmaline - Protection
Black Tourmaline is a crystal that cleanses, purifies, and transforms heavy energy into light energy. It helps you to ground yourself and protects and balances your aura. It is a powerful mental healer as it turns negative thoughts into positive ones and allows you to release stress, obsessive thoughts and bring balance and harmony into your life.

It is an excellent crystal to have in your room or carry around with you as it will take in any negative energy and release positive energy. It also forms a shield of protection.

Caribbean Calcite - Communication with spirit
Caribbean Calcite opens your channels to communicate with spirit, whether that is your Angels, Guides, or loved ones in spirit. It helps balance the higher chakras (throat, brow, and crown) to express your feelings and thoughts with more clarity enhancing your connection with the spirit world. Caribbean Calcite increases your psychic abilities, so it works wonderfully with your solar plexus. It continually improves communication with those in the higher realms. It is a beautiful crystal, it is calming, and it helps to soothe the sensitivities.

Chevron Amethyst - Spiritual - Protection - Best version of yourself - Strength - Courage
Chevron Amethyst is an excellent crystal to help you to find peace within yourself, peace of mind. It helps you utterly understand you and what works for you, what brings you joy, what you need to release from an opposing point of view, and help you be the best version of yourself. It is also a protection crystal, cleanses your aura, and lifts your vibration higher. It enhances your energy fields to keep you well and keep your well-being as highest it can. It helps you in finding your inner strength and courage. It is a calming, soothing crystal and is known to help you sleep. It opens your third eye and crown chakra, allowing you to connect to your intuition and spiritual wisdom. It is also known as the crystal of spirituality.

Dendritic Agate - Peace - Confidence - Protection - Abundance - Prosperity
Dendritic Agate is a crystal of peace, peace to your mind, body, and soul. Wants to create tranquillity within your

surroundings. It is a crystal of development and growth. It helps your self-confidence and perseverance and transforms negative energies (both in the environment and the body) into positive energies. To enable you to find that inner strength and stability to move forward with that project you are working on. Also known for abundance and prosperity, not just monetary, but in every aspect of one's life.

Dumortierite - Healing - Headaches - Studying
Dumortierite is a crystal that opens the third eye chakra and is excellent for your mind. It wants to reduce stress in your body and calm your mind and those energies that create anxiety. Dumortierite can alleviate headaches and brings you clarity. It is a fantastic crystal for students, studying or learning as it stimulates the mind. It is an excellent crystal to meditate with and can help clear blockages in your chakras.

Fluorite - Helps the mind - Grounding - In the now
Putting Fluorite in your pocket or wearing it can help you focus your mind and motivate you to move forward. It helps to give strength and stability, de-clutter your mind and will get rid of anything negative. It works with the third eye chakra and is an excellent crystal to meditate with as it offers protection and helps with dreaming. It also helps to ground you but keeps you in the higher vibration, keeping you focused and keeping you in the now. It can help you if you suffer from dizziness and vertigo.

Labradorite - Spiritual Growth - Magic - Trust in spirit
Labradorite is a crystal of magic. It is an immensely powerful crystal to use in psychic development as it helps enhance psychic abilities. It is a crystal of transformation as it opens the higher

chakras, the throat, brow, and the crown, enabling you to trust your intuition and trust the messages you are receiving from your Angels, Guides, and loved ones in spirit. It helps you believe in yourselves and your capabilities that you can communicate with spirit. This crystal helps homes your ability to trust that you can hear through signs, feeling, and thoughts of what spirit is guiding you.

It is a must-have crystal for mediums, psychics, shamans, or anyone that works spiritually.

Lapis Lazuli - Healing headaches - Spiritual enlightenment - Improving relationships
Lapis Lazuli is beautiful for in stealing within you that deep sense of compassion for yourselves and others. It enhances your ability to communicate and to be open and honest with those around us. It is beautiful to inspire deeper relationships, deeper connections and enables you to have beautiful open, honest, and caring relationships with your love ones and your friends. It helps you to connect deeper within yourself and supports spiritual enlightenment. It allows you to find your divine purpose. It can help with migraines and headaches by placing it on the forehead and imagining a blue ray of light going into your third eye.

Larimar - Communication - Finding your path - Healing
Larimar resonates with your throat chakra, enabling you to speak with clarity and express your emotions and thoughts. Beautiful Larimar helps if you are feeling lost or wondering what your soul or life purpose is. It enables you to understand your path, allows you to acknowledge the way forward with appreciation, and moves your alignment with your higher self. This delicate crystal helps to release any blockages up through your crown.

Mangano Calcite - Self-love - Healing

Mangano Calcite is one of the most beautiful crystals to helps you love yourself, enables you to nurture yourself, and is like having a big loving hug. It encourages you to accept love and have self-love, and act lovingly towards others. It helps you to take time for yourself whether you want to sit and be doing nothing. You are allowed to enjoy now and then being, put your feet up. It makes you focus on that beautiful energy of love and self-love. It is a calming crystal that eases and heals your heart chakra.

Merlinite - Magic - Self-discovery - Spiritual Growth - Forgiveness

Merlinite gets it is named from the wizard Merlin; it attracts good luck and draws the magic of the universe synchronicity. It is an excellent crystal to use for psychic development as it opens your third eye and helps develop your psychic abilities. It enhances your connection to the spiritual realms and allows you to trust your intuition.

In meditation, it can help with past life regression. It can help connect you to animals, nature, plants, as well as other spiritual beings. It enables you to understand yourself on a much deeper level, including those aspects you do not like about yourself. It awakens you to your true self, accepting both light and your shadow side, which helps you with forgiveness and what you need to work on. It balances all the chakras and will bring you on a journey of self-discovery.

Moonstone – New beginnings - Feminine power - Finding yourself - Success

Moonstone is a crystal for "new beginnings," Moonstone is a

crystal of inner growth and strength. It soothes emotions and stress, providing calmness and peace. Moonstone enhances your feminine power as it connects to your inner goddess. It improves your intuition as it activates the third eye chakra and the crown chakra and clears your aura. It promotes inspiration, success, and good fortune in love and business matters.

Moonstone is the crystal of the High Priestess and represents femininity. It has a strong connection to the moon and is an excellent crystal to meditate with as it brings you deep into your inner selves and will help you find the hidden part of you that you have lost. The energy of this crystal connects to the moon, which makes it a powerful crystal. The cycles of the moon have a substantial effect on Mother Earth and its inhabitants. The moon reminds you to be aware of the cycles of your life. Each time you complete a cycle, it takes you on to a higher level of wisdom, understanding, and self-awareness.

Morganite - New love - Healing heart
Morganite resonates with your heart chakra and wants to calm, soothe, and reassure. It helps release feelings of resentment, anger, annoyance, and irritations and bring you healing energy, compassion, joy, confidence, inner strength, self-respect, and unconditional love. It invites in love enabling you to have beautiful relationships with those around you. If you are looking for new love, it will attract love to you.

Moss Agate - New beginnings - Healing - Successful - Boost self-esteem
Moss Agate is a crystal of new beginnings. It refreshes your soul and enables you to see the beauty in yourself and all around you, it helps you believe in yourself. It is also a natural anti-

231

defamatory. If you feel pain or discomfort, place your crystal in that area or put it in your pocket, as it will help. Moss Agate wants to gently reduce your sensitivity, especially if some harshness surrounds you. This crystal helps to attract abundance and improves your self-esteem making you more successful in whatever you are doing.

Opalite - Communication - Persistent - Love
Opalite is excellent for assisting all forms of communication. It helps to bring up hidden feelings that we do not recognise within yourselves, enabling you to communicate those feelings with love and dignity. It is a crystal of persistence. If you have a feeling, you are not achieving, Opalite will help to see you through it. It also helps with change and transformation. It is also known as the crystal of love and rewards faithful lovers to form lasting romantic bonds.

Orac Agate - Go with the Flow - Healing - Forgiveness
Orac Agate wants to help you to go with the flow. It allows you to utterly understand your issues that you are holding onto, preventing you from living in your own peace. Orca Agate is a healing crystal that can help you heal any deep, emotional wounds, thus allowing you to forgive yourself and others.

Pink Opal - Love - Healing the heart - Releasing old wounds
Pink Opal is a powerful crystal for healing your emotions. It resonates with the heart chakra and aids in emotional balance and healing matters of the heart. It is kind to your heart, it wants to love and cherish your heart, it wants to heal your heart. Pink Opal wants to console, calm, and heal any hurt or grief you are holding onto. It encourages your heart to release fear, worry, and anxiety.

It helps to release hurt and stress, bringing peace, calmness, and tranquillity to the heart. It focuses your energy on love, and love is, of course, the greatest healer.

Prasiolite Quartz - Success - Prosperity - Abundance - Healing

Prasiolite Quartz resonates with the heart chakra and wants to balance your heart chakra's energies, releasing sadness and old hurt, bringing in joy. It is a beautiful crystal for enhancing creativity, helping you with your projects. It is a crystal for success, prosperity, and abundance.

Pyrite - Protection - Foresight - Trusting the universe

Pyrite is a powerful protection crystal that shields and protects you against all forms of negative energy, physically and emotionally. It stimulates the mind bringing you clarity and enhances your memory function. It is enabling you to recall relevant information when needed.

It helps you see the bigger picture rather than what is just going on in front of you. Helping you to act accordingly, taking you away from a place of fear or insecurity, enabling you to trust the universe is working as it needs to and that all is well in your world. It is also a crystal of abundance.

Red Howlite - Emotions - Nurture relationships with females Spiritual growth

Red Howlite is useful for reducing anxiety, tensions, stress, and anger, especially when surrounded by people on the negative side. It is a soothing, calming, and gentle crystal, and it resonates with the Root Chakra. Hence, it helps you nurture yourself and encourage others to nurture their relationships with other females, such as mothers, sisters, or friends.

Meditating with Red Howlite, you improve your link with the higher realm to your Spiritual Family.

Red Tiger Eye - Spiritual Growth - Grounding - Passion - Sexual issues

Red Tiger Eye helps bring higher and divine energy into your physical selves, rooting in your root chakra, grounding you to mother earth, and helping you feel more balanced and more connected to the higher realms. It lifts your vitality and gives you motivation.

If you are feeling bored or tired, pop some in your pocket as it raises your level of passion, it takes you forwards in a way that makes you feel more balanced. It is a stimulating crystal and can support motivation and a more active sex drive. Use Red Tige Eye with the Root Chakra to ground sexual ideas into the physical world or resolve sexual issues that cause problems in a relationship.

Rose Quartz - Love - Love yourself – Fertility - Healing

Rose Quartz is the crystal of universal love, it promotes unconditional love, particularly self-love, and improves relationships, especially romantic relationships. It will activate and open your heart chakra, which allows you to connect to your heart and find ways to accept and love yourself and others. It can help you understand and get past situations, allowing your heart to heal from emotional wounds such as heartbreak and help you feel like you can trust in love again. It brings your heart back into balance with its gentle, pink energy.

It resonates with the heart chakra, so any problems around the chest area will help the healing process. It can help promote fertility, so if you wish to have a baby, this crystal will help you conceive. If you are pregnant, carrying it or wearing this crystal will protect you and the baby during pregnancy. It is also good for the skin, making an elixir, pop it into your water and drink the water will help give you a beautiful glow and improve your skin.

Septarian - Grounding - Patients - Protection
Septarian is an extremely powerful but delicate crystal. It gives you a feeling of hugging you. It is excellent for transmitting negative energy, pessimistic feelings, horrible thoughts into something lighter and more positive. Septarian is a grounding crystal that helps you to allow for better tolerance and patience. It provides reassurance and comfort that all is well in your world.

Serpentine - Spiritual Connection - Healing
Serpentine naturally raises your consciousness, enabling you to connect to the divine, your Spiritual Family. It is a beautiful crystal to meditate with as it opens your higher chakras to help you feel connected to the higher realms. It a natural healing crystal, it enhances the body's own natural healing ability to heal itself. It can help to recover if you suffer from diabetes and hypoglycemia.

Sodalite - Spiritual Growth - Believe in yourself - Helps grief.
Sodalite is a beautiful crystal to open your chakras, improve intuition, and connect to divine energies. It opens your chakra to receiving divine love helping you to feel connected to your Angels, Guides, and your love ones in spirit. Sodalite alleviates your journey to your inner self and allows you to believe in yourself. It gives you the confidence to speak out. This crystal also helps soothe grief and mourning as it enables you to connect and communicate with your loved ones in spirit, and lastly, this crystal is fantastic to alleviate pain in any way.

Sunset Aura Quartz - Joy - Let Go - Positivity

Sunset Aura Quartz helps clears feelings of resentment and grief, those lower energies that prevent you from moving forwards, those energies that make you feel stuck. For that reason, it also helps you let go of unhealthy relationships, dysfunctional relationships, and negative relationships that may hold you back. It can help you have a sense of freedom, releasing, enabling you to move forward to be with people who are more in alignment with yourself. Stunning Aura Quartz stimulates all your chakras so that you can feel more confident in all that you do and allows you to be creative.

It raises your vibration energy, giving you a positive outlook on life and enhances you to find joy in everyday life, sunshine, birds singing.

Tiger Eye - Good luck - Success - Protection - Working with the universe

Tiger Eye is the crystal for good luck. It helps to bring clarity to your mind and emotions, helping you be objective in facing and overcoming obstacles and difficulties. It allows you to gain a better understanding of yourself and harmonises what you want in life. This means you can succeed in the things you want or need to achieve.

It is a protective crystal and helps to re-energise your body. It lifts your energies to deal with everyday life, enabling the universe to respond positively.

Unakite - Healing - Grounding - Now - Dreams

Unakite is a healing crystal, particularly useful to use when recovering from an illness, which will help your healing process. It will bring healing to your heart and gives you the courage to be you. It balances the mind, emotions, and the spiritual body and grounds your spiritual aspect of who you are into mother earth. Unakite is excellent to meditate with as it will help you still yourself and be in the now. It makes you feel aligned and re-energised with your higher self and enables you to let go of any emotional pain you may hold onto.

It works with your third eye, connects to your visions, and dreams, and reminds you not to let fear destroy your dreams.